Prais

Choosing
Learning to Love

Growing into gratitude comes in discrete pieces: coming to see "calamity" as a deepening experience, as well as recognizing that one already has enough. The culmination of this gem of a book is the account of the author's brother's learning how to say "thank you" in the face of his inevitable death. Like a slow-building formation, James Autry's wisdom regarding gratitude slowly builds into insight that repeatedly appears just when needed.

—JOHN MAGUIRE
President Emeritus
Claremont Graduate University

Jim Autry does it again. In his usual winsome and witty way, Autry reminds us that our posture toward daily life—on both good days and bad—ought to be one of gratitude. With just the right blend of humor and heart, his stories, poems, and reflections all serve to help us develop and nurture our own spirit of gratitude.

—DAVID W. MILLER
Director, Princeton University Faith & Work Initiative

Jim Autry is a very wise soul. His inspiring stories, observations, and suggestions are helpful in living a life full of gratitude. This is a very worthwhile read.

—PETER ROY
Co-author *The Book of Hard Choices*
Former President of Whole Foods Market

Amidst the pressures life thrusts upon us, the notion of making a choice to express—no, to live—gratitude may seem naive. But it is profound, and in beautiful story form and moving poetry we are led to see how gratitude doesn't isolate us from the rough-and-tumble of the world, but rather actually helps us engage it more richly. Several of the chapters were so powerful that I found myself in tears, agreeing that each of us indeed has much for which to be grateful.

—DAVID TRICKETT
President of Iliff School of Theology
Denver, Colorado

I experience gratitude as a deep feeling of joy and sorrow as one, of being present to the world. Jim's book captures this experience—it is filled with moments of joy and sorrow, offering us a profound recognition of what life is. I'm so grateful for this book.

—MARGARET J. WHEATLEY
Author, *Leadership and the New Science* and other books

CHOOSING GRATITUDE

LEARNING TO LOVE
THE LIFE YOU HAVE

Smyth & Helwys Publishing, Inc.
6316 Peake Road
Macon, Georgia 31210-3960
1-800-747-3016

The paper used in this publication meets the minimum requirements of
American National Standard for Information Sciences—
Permanence of Paper for Printed Library Materials.
ANSI Z39.48–1984. (alk. paper)

Library of Congress Cataloging-in-Publication Data

Autry, James A.
Choosing gratitude : learning to love the life you have / by James A. Autry.
p. cm.
ISBN 978-1-57312-614-4 (alk. paper)
1. Gratitude--Religious aspects--Christianity. I. Title.
BV4647.G8A96 2012
241'.4--dc23

2011049213

CHOOSING

Learning to Love the Life You Have

GRATITUDE

James A. Autry

Also by James A. Autry

Books

Looking Around for God: The Oddly Reverent Observations of an Unconventional Christian

The Book of Hard Choices (with Peter Roy)

The Servant Leader: How to Build a Creative Team, Develop Great Morale, and Improve Bottom Line Performance

The Spirit of Retirement

Real Power: Business Lessons from the Tao Te Ching (with Stephen Mitchell)

Confessions of an Accidental Businessman

Life & Work: A Manager's Search for Meaning

Love & Profit: The Art of Caring Leadership

Poetry

Nights under a Tin Roof: Recollections of a Southern Boyhood

Life after Mississippi

Videos

Love & Profit

Life & Work

The Spirit of Work

To my dear friends,
the Bargers,
for whom my gratitude
is almost beyond expression.

Acknowledgments

No one writes a book without a lot of support from others, and I must begin by acknowledging my wife, Sally Pederson. I can't describe what she has to put up with when I'm working on a book. Fortunately for me, she is the most optimistic and good-natured person I've ever met.

Next, my friends Wes Graham and Virginia Traxler have listened to essays and poetry and have made helpful comments. Oldest friends Sam Gore and Jim Ferguson let me write their stories. A special thank you to Angie Witmer for letting me share part of her story.

And of course, I acknowledge and appreciate the good people at Smyth & Helwys, especially Keith Gammons. It is so refreshing and, yes, inspiring to work with business people who practice the ethics they profess.

—JAA

Contents

Section Seven: The Gratitude Inventory

Preface

A few months ago, after I returned from my early-morning "gratitude walk," and sat down with a cup of coffee and the morning newspaper, I thought, "How in the world can anyone look at the newspaper these days or watch the news on television and then find gratitude in the midst of all this mess?"

Yet I had just spent an hour of sheer gratitude doing nothing but walking. You might think I simply shut out the world. To the contrary, I opened myself to the world we don't read or hear about on the news, a world that's available to us all the time.

It is easy to get caught up in economics and politics, and, indeed, those things have an impact on our lives, but I fear too many of us are becoming obsessed with the political and economic world "out there." We are letting the problems of the world push in on us to the point that we begin to see them as our personal problems. We let them define how we live and what we think and what we talk about.

And it seems to me that we're also letting those things keep us a bit angry all the time. It's not healthy for the country, and it's certainly not healthy for us as individuals.

I'm not suggesting we shouldn't care about our country and its people or ignore our responsibility to be informed and to participate in the process. We simply need to realize that overly zealous participation in the economic, political, and social issues of the day can make us lose focus on the things that create a balanced life. I see it all the time; so do you.

Part of the result is that, in the quest for change, in the desire for more of something, in our anger about what the world is not and what we don't have, we lose sight of how the world is, how our lives are, and what we have. When we do that, we've lost the gift and blessing of gratitude.

I am also not suggesting that this little book will save you from the pressures of the world. I know that the world is with us. I am suggesting that perhaps sharing my stories and reflections can help you transcend the pressures and stay in touch with the people and experiences that really matter, and have mattered, in your life. As you read, I hope you will remember the things for which you can truly be grateful.

Introduction

Gratitude doesn't come naturally. We have to learn it.

You'd think we'd be born grateful, helpless as we are coming into the world depending on someone else for everything. Instead, from the first moment, we demand what we need. Then, within a few years, our needs are taken for granted and we turn our attention to the things we want, whether we need them or not. We learn that we can no longer demand, so we beg, wheedle, and cajole until we get what we want.

The first tiny step toward gratitude is when our parents teach us to say, "Thank you."

Some of us never get past that. Some of us simply grow up to be well-behaved children, only older. Give us something or do something for us, and we say, "Thank you" or, in some parts of the country, "Appreciate it" or "Much obliged." Polite, conditioned responses, but not gratitude.

Don't misunderstand; I appreciate polite expressions. They help to lubricate the gears of social concourse and are part of what we consider civilized behavior.

But gratitude is something altogether different. Learning gratitude is a spiritual, not a social, process. Not only is it not conditioned behavior; it's not behavior at all. It's a deeply ingrained aspect of our consciousness, an attitude, a condition that, when learned and practiced, becomes fundamental to our being. No doubt it is made evident as behavior, but it is not behavior itself. We can be polite, courteous, respectful, helpful, and all the attributes found in the Boy Scout law, and still not have gratitude.

This is because gratitude, if we have it at all, exists within ourselves and is measured only by ourselves. Like meditation, it has a singular benefit. We can't give it to anyone else. And we can never expect anyone else to say, "He sure has gratitude" or "She is a grateful person." People may say, "He is giving and unselfish" or "She is so courteous and respectful of others," but they can't say, "Doesn't her gratitude give you a good feeling?"

You are the only one who knows that gratitude is fundamental to who you are. To paraphrase an old saying, gratitude is its own reward.

But doesn't gratitude affect behavior? Of course. If gratitude is essential to who you are, then you will always be quick to express appreciation for someone's help and to respond in kind. That becomes second nature, but let's go a little deeper. It's easy enough to say "Thank you" or "I appreciate your help," but it's not so easy to feel gratitude when someone has disappointed you, has failed to help, has withheld good will, or has deliberately been obstructive. When you have learned gratitude and fully internalized it so that it becomes who you are, your response is not resentment or ill feelings in return. Instead, it is gratitude that you are not diminished by the other's attitudes or actions and that you have the knowledge and emotional resources to take the next step. The next step may be an assertive response, but whatever it is, do it without ill will or an attitude of revenge.

To be sure, plenty of circumstances in life challenge our commitment to gratitude, but a lifestyle of gratitude means cultivating a spirit of thankfulness through the negatives of life—sickness, death of loved ones, divorce, and so on—and remember that there will always be more reasons for gratitude than for despair. (See section 6 for insights into how one man lived in gratitude as he faced cancer and death.)

Gratitude is the best attitude. Gratitude is the sign of noble souls.

—Aesop (620–550 bc)

Looking at another aspect of how gratitude affects behavior, consider the current discussions about the "psychology of scarcity" versus the "psychology of abundance," the debate between those who feel there's not enough for everyone—so it's important to protect themselves—and those who feel there can be enough for all.

It sometimes strikes me that Americans are preoccupied with what we don't have rather than with what we do have. Like many consumers, I struggle with this. Will I have enough for retirement? Will my wife have enough after I die? What if some terrible condition or accident eats up our savings? I've planned well, and by any reasonable measurement, my family and I have no worries, yet the scarcity demons creep in and keep me awake. These anxieties are the enemy of gratitude.

To remind myself always to return to gratitude, I have a sentence scripted in fancy calligraphy on my office bulletin board: "What You Have Is Enough." Indeed, if you live in gratitude, your attitude is always that what you have is enough. Whatever it is, it is enough.

Yet gratitude goes beyond what's enough for you and yours. Gratitude may lead to generosity for which other people express gratitude to you, but your own gratitude comes from *their* generosity in allowing you to help.

This spirit of gratitude extends beyond your relationships with people to include your relationship with the natural world. Eventually, you will begin to see everything with new eyes.

Nurturing a spirit of gratitude is not easy. It is a choice. You have to decide that this is how you want to be and then commit yourself to being that way. There is no checklist for growing in gratitude. Just as it's not about behavior, it's also not about what to do; it's about how to be. Being—not doing. This is not about a simple change of attitude; it's about a complete shift in consciousness. It becomes an internal discipline almost like meditation or centering prayer. The external world doesn't change, but your awareness of it does. Thus your response to the world changes.

Perhaps the greatest response comes in the realization that everything that has happened in the history of the world comes down to this moment, and that every such moment accumulates into the life you have now. If you can fill your life with moments of gratitude, then you will love the life you have.

In closing, I express my gratitude to you for giving me the opportunity to share my reflections, observations, and stories. The Kansas poet William Stafford once said that it is the writer's work to dig so deep into his own story that he reaches everyone's story. I hope this book succeeds in doing that and, in the process, perhaps helps you on your own journey of gratitude.

Section One

For One Thing and Another

The Gratitude Walk

I'm a walker. I have been for a long time. But in the past few years, the nature of my walks has changed. I don't mean the physical nature—I still just put one foot after another—but the emotional and spiritual nature.

For years I would start walking and, before I knew it, my brain would slip from "relax" mode to "worry" mode. I usually walk in the morning, soon after reading the newspaper, thus I worried about the wars, the jihadists, the economic crisis and the healthcare crisis and the education crisis. Before I knew it, I'd stopped focusing on the pleasures of walking my neighborhood with its many trees and flower gardens and had worked myself into a state of high anxiety about the world.

I knew that walking was supposed to be good for my health; I also knew that stress and worry were supposed to be bad for my health. So, I wondered, was one canceling out the other? Of course it was. There is nothing healthy about exercising the body while worrying yourself to death. And that goes for spiritual health as well.

But how could I change? How could I get out of the "worry" mode and into the "relax" mode? Perhaps the most futile effort in the world is to try to make yourself relax. You certainly can't talk yourself into it, as if you could somehow make such a compelling argument that you'd simply take a deep breath and relax. You can't command yourself as if giving a military command: "Ready . . . relax!"

My wife said, "Try praying as you walk." That's always a good suggestion, of course, so the next time I walked out the door, I was ready to do as many people do and run through a laundry list of things

I needed to pray for, not just for myself but for the world. Unfortunately, my prayers tended to leave me in a discontented frame of mind as I went through my list of concerns. After praying, the anxieties began to creep back into my consciousness, and the next thing I knew I was obsessing about the same stuff again. It didn't help to tell myself that I should leave it all to God.

Then one morning after a night of spring thunderstorms, I opened the door and walked into fresh, fragrant air and the sound of birdsong. I stretched to limber up, then took a deep breath and involuntarily said, "Thank you." At that moment, I remembered Meister Eckhardt's admonition, "In praying, it is enough to say thank you."

That was several years ago, and it was the beginning of what I call my gratitude walk. I realized that I was grateful for that morning and that I'd been grateful for other mornings but had not recognized or articulated my gratitude. I vowed it would be different from then on.

And it has been. Every time I do the morning walk, I make it a walking meditation of gratitude. And when my mind tries to shift gears into some other thought, I immediately take a breath and express gratitude for something or someone. I always say it aloud to myself (not too loudly, of course; I don't want to become the neighborhood's doddering old fool).

Like so many things, though, the gratitude walk is not as easy as it sounds. If you decide to try it yourself, you may be surprised as you get started by how challenging it is to come up with an hour's worth of gratitude. I began with family and friends and then named them one by one. That was obvious and easy, but I realized soon enough that I didn't have enough family and friends to last for even a thirty-minute walk. More important, I realized that, in taking such a structured approach, I was in danger of turning the experience into yet another stress-inducing chore.

I needed to *feel* gratitude, not *think* gratitude. I needed to stop working at it and instead be open to it and let it come to me as naturally and effortlessly as breathing.

So I evolved toward what I think of as the next level of the gratitude walk. I asked the question, "What am I truly grateful for?" Then, rather than running through a list, I simply walked and waited for the answers to come. And they did.

What answers came? Life, for one thing. You don't have to be my age to be grateful for being alive. The abundance of nature, for another. Just as on that spring morning after the thunderstorms, I felt surrounded by blessings for which to be grateful.

And while the walk took on the aspects of a spiritual practice like prayer or meditation, it didn't require a big spiritual insight. I just had to realize that, like a lot of people, I take too much for granted. I had to learn to look at the everydayness of this walk with new eyes.

For instance, I often say I'm grateful for a certain line of sycamore trees and how the sun hits them, for a particular bird song, for a mother pushing a stroller, for the smell of a fresh-cut lawn. I can laugh with gratitude at squirrels chasing one another in their great mating ritual or at the robins dive-bombing my cat to keep him away from their nest. There's almost nothing in nature I can't be grateful for (although mosquitoes and chiggers come close).

I'm not sure what the next phase is, but I think it is probably learning to apply the gratitude walk to every other part of my life, and to learn to live in gratitude no matter where I am or what I'm doing.

I recommend the gratitude walk. It doesn't take the place of prayer or meditation, but it's a wonderful way to help integrate your mind, body, and spirit, not to mention a refreshing way to start or end the day.

But I say again that it is not as easy as it may sound. It takes commitment and practice, but so does anything else worth pursuing. It is one of the little steps that have changed my life, and I suspect it could change yours too.

The Trouble with Aging

Here's what I've learned about aging.

It's important to honor your memories of the places, experiences, and people that helped make you what you are in this life.

It's equally important not to let those memories hold you hostage to the past and keep you from living your life today.

As I write this, I've just returned from two reunions, one a gathering of former Air Force fighter pilots and the other my high school class reunion.

At the Air Force reunion, there was joy and storytelling, "hangar flying," camaraderie. We remembered old friends now dead, some killed in the profession of flying and some victims of pernicious diseases. At the concluding dinner, we said our goodbyes, knowing that some of us won't be there for the next one. It was, as always, bittersweet.

Last week I went to Memphis, Tennessee, to be with people I hardly know but with whom I share the experience of Memphis Tech High School, class of 1951. We began with an informal gathering at one of the old barbecue places, Leonard's, now in a big mall. We sat at tables and talked of when we sat in cars and fondled one another in the dim light behind the original Leonard's drive-in a long time ago.

What struck me in both of these experiences was the presence of people who were still holding on to the past of their imaginations. I understand that; I think it's always tempting to look back in fondness at times that seem better than these times. For the pilots, it was a great adventure, perhaps the greatest adventure of their lives. And for some of the high school class members, particularly those who held

offices or were sports stars or cheer-
leaders, it may have been the only
time in which they were held in high
esteem by their peers.

I don't know why they hang on as
they do, but at some level I understand it. What happens is that the
memories keep accumulating and
building up to the extent that they

*Gratitude is not only
the greatest of
virtues, but the
parent of all the
others.*

—MARCUS TULLIUS CICERO
(106 BC–43 BC)

begin to crowd out the present. And memory becomes then the greatest and most addictive means of time travel. You get a glimpse of
something, anything, or you hear a song, and it triggers a sequence
that plays out in your memory like a film retrieved from the image
library of the past.

I often think about people I love, yet I know that I would not be
able to spend much time with them now and probably would not
much enjoy the time I did spend with them. I guess it must be that
I love them for who they were and not for who they are, for what they
meant to me then, not now. But I don't want to let go. It would be
like betraying the memory of the friendship we once had.

It has become a cliché of aging that we can remember in exquisite
detail names of people or experiences from years ago, but we can't
recall whom we met or what we did yesterday. I experience it myself
and have come to take it as a reminder of the need to realize that, at
the time when I was living the experiences that now give me such rich
memories, I probably did not consider them so "rich." It was just
everyday life. The passage of time somehow changed my perception of
the past and imbued it with a quality it probably never had. In other
words, I'm sure I romanticize my past, and I suspect we all do that to
some extent.

Why? Was our past better than our present?

Know what I think? It is not that the past was better but that
somehow we think our lives then had more meaning than our present
lives. Not more fun, not more adventure, but more meaning.

But it's not true. Just as we need to avoid becoming hostage to our
memories, we need to realize that we are creating new memories every

day. If we are conscious of that, we can also find meaning in what we do every day.

So here's the truth:

The past is important. Our past is important.

Our memories are important.

Former friendships are important.

Realizing that the dead live on in our memories and thus live on in our lives is important.

But the most important thing is to embrace the present, to love our lives today—even if there are physical and intellectual challenges—and to understand that we have the power to imbue everything we do, every relationship we have, and every day that we live with meaning.

Thanks for the Memory

One recent morning, I got up, read the newspaper, ate breakfast, delivered a jacket to my son's house, and lay back down and dozed off. When I awoke, I asked my wife, "What day is this?"

She told me.

Then we went into the kitchen. When I saw the newspaper, I asked, "Have I read the newspaper?"

"Yes," she said.

"Have I had breakfast?"

"Yes," she said again, but by this time she was concerned. I had lost my memory of what I'd done, and I write this, including the conversation above, not based on memory but on my wife's story of the day.

She drove me to the emergency room, where the doctors and nurses, thinking I might have had a stroke, put me through a battery of tests— MRI, MRA, EEG, and CT scan. The neurologist asked questions like, "What day is this?" "What month is this?" "Who is president of the United States?" and so on. I couldn't answer any of them.

Rejoice evermore.
Pray without ceasing.
In everything give
thanks: for this is the
will of God.

—Saint Paul of Tarsus
1 Thess 5:16-18 (AD 54)

Thus began a day completely lost to memory. The diagnosis: transient global amnesia. It is not uncommon, and according to the data is not a precursor to stroke or dementia. It is a temporary loss of short-term memory, lasting usually no longer than twenty-four hours.

My memory had returned by the next morning, although I could not remember being brought to the hospital, going through any of the tests, or anything else from the previous day. It was a day wiped from my memory.

Where would I begin with the gratitude? The medical people, of course. But most of all, my wife who stayed with me, calmly answering my many questions over and over again. I'd say, "Sally, please answer these questions. Why did you bring me here? What were my symptoms? Give me a time line."

Within five or ten minutes after she carefully answered them, I'd say, "Sally, please answer these questions," and repeat the whole thing over again. She told me it was like the movie *Groundhog Day*. We've laughed about it since—but it wasn't funny at the time.

The episode made me exceedingly grateful for my memory and, at the same time, intensified my concern for the many people whose memory, for one reason or another, leaves and does not return.

A Visit to the White House

I was invited to the White House in the summer of 1990, and I felt right at home there.

But it was not in the way that all Americans should be able to feel at home at the White House; it was in another way. I felt at home with people who hobbled in braces and on crutches, with people on rolling hospital beds, with people who spoke in sign language, and with people who, with their misshapen bodies, struggled to speak and to push the buttons and levers on their self-propelled wheelchairs. And I felt especially at home with children whose behavior was often strange and unpredictable like the behavior of my son, Ronald, age six at the time, who has autism.

We were gathered—these disabled people plus many of us considered by society not to be disabled—for the signing of the Americans with Disabilities Act on July 26, 1990. Not since the passage of public law 94-142, the Education of All Handicapped Children Act in the 1970s, had there been a law this significant for disabled people.

And in that mass of 2,000 people on the south lawn, every face was glowing with a joy the newly freed slaves must have felt after the Emancipation Proclamation. After years of suffering the most systematic discrimination in our history, disabled people were about to become free at last.

At the time, I had done volunteer work in the disability community for about twenty years, but I was not prepared for the scene at the White House. The minute I entered the southwest gate, I could not contain my tears. All I could do was scribble in my notebook. Some excerpts follow.

There is joy here, a sense of victory, a sense of hope amid promise, a sense of empowerment. Empowerment to do what? Only to live, to work, to participate, to prove their worth to society—and to themselves.

Everyone is smiles and cameras. I notice that the hearing-impaired people can use sign to communicate over the noise of the crowd. Those of us dependent on sound can't be heard above the roar. . . .

In the midst of all this, I think of Ronald and of Sally [my wife, who at the time was president of the Autism Society of Iowa] and wish they were here.

The M.C. tells everyone to clear the aisles so we can begin. I have news for the M.C.: it has already begun. This train is moving and the officials better just jump on board. . .

The senators arrive. Tom Harkin, to great applause. Bob Dole with his withered hand, moving among the wheelchairs. Orrin Hatch, Bob Michel, Ted Kennedy. Everyone seems to be on the same side of the political aisle today. . .

Tony Coelho shows up. Despite the scandal, the disabled people applaud him vigorously—they know he has epilepsy and they know of his work on this bill.

The president and Mrs. George H. W. Bush enter to wild cheering and applause. . .

Looking back at the president, I notice the press corps. They look bored, almost cynical. They are laughing and joking, and I think, of course this has been staged, and it is a "photo op," and there are reasons to doubt the sincerity of some of the politicians— but I'll take it because its importance to these disabled people far transcends the rest of that stuff.

The Rev. Mr. Harold Wilke, who has no arms, invokes in his prayer the passage, "Let my people go," and prays that the chains of slavery for millions of disabled people will finally be broken.

President Bush then rose to speak and said to the crowd, "This day belongs to you." The people went wild again. The president pointed out that the United States was the first country in the world to pass such a law, and he said he was sure many countries would now follow suit.

It was a good speech. He referred to the Berlin Wall, and then, as he picked up a pen, he said, "Now as I sign this legislation, we take a sledgehammer to another wall . . . let the shameful wall of exclusion come tumbling down."

When the president rose to leave, he bent over to the legendary advocate for disability rights, Justin Dart, proud and smiling in a wheelchair, and, it being too awkward to shake Dart's hand, he kissed him on the forehead.

> *Men are more ready to repay an injury than a benefit because gratitude is a burden and revenge a pleasure.*
>
> —TACITUS (AD 56–120)

It was more moving than some of us grown men could take. I made a final note: "88 degrees. Tears. Sweat. Joy. Triumph. Suddenly I see the only empty chair in the whole crowd. I had not even noticed, yet it is right next to me. And I think of Ronald and know in my heart that the seat was saved for him."

Talk about gratitude . . .

(Adapted from *Life and Work, A Manager's Search for Meaning*)

In Praise of Dog Parks

I was tempted to title this "Everything I know about community I learned at the dog park," but that would be an overstatement. Still, there are a lot of good lessons to be learned there.

My wife and I have been caring for our "grand-dog" while our son is on a weekend trip. Part of the responsibility is taking Gilda (the Corgi) to the dog park where she can indulge her herding instincts by running with the other dogs while we humans hang out and watch.

A little community develops among the humans because, I think, we all have something on which we agree: Dogs are good. We don't talk about politics or war or sports or television or movies; we talk about our dogs, and we demonstrate acceptance and good will by petting one another's dogs. What a respite that is from our everyday concourse. It makes me want to suggest that every member of Congress must be accompanied by a dog. (No pit bulls allowed; Congress has enough of those already.)

My young friend with a seizure disorder has a helper dog that senses when she is about to have a seizure, then guides her to a safe place and makes her sit down. A miracle dog.

Perhaps dogs could be trained to sense anger or hostile confrontation, and when a congressperson was about to sound off, they could push the person to sit back down and cool off.

Maybe not, but if congresspeople even had to take their dogs to the congressional dog park and pick up the animal waste in a little plastic bag and deposit it in the garbage, that would be a great lesson in service and in humility, both of which are needed these days.

They might also learn some lessons from the dogs at the dog park.

For instance, the dogs pay no attention to size or color or breed. When a new dog arrives, they rush to greet it with great excitement. All are welcome. They don't form cliques. They sniff one another equally and without prejudice. (One of the men at our dog park, channeling Jerry Lee Lewis, quipped, "Whole lotta sniffin' goin' on.")

> *No duty is more urgent than that of returning thanks.*
>
> —SAINT AMBROSE (AD 340–397)

And when one of the humans throws a ball, any dog that chooses to chase it does so. They obviously love being together, and when their humans call them to leave, the dogs obey with great reluctance.

I like to think they have some way of communicating that we don't understand and they're saying things like, "Gotta go, gotta keep my human happy, see you next Saturday," and so on.

As for the humans, I hope that when we leave the dog park we have learned the lessons and are calmer, more open to other people, and more accepting of differences.

I once heard a man say that his ambition was to be as good a person as his dog thinks he is. Not a bad goal for any of us, including congresspeople.

Teenage Magic

Several years ago, I accompanied my son Ronald on what turned out to be a magical mystery tour in which I witnessed a transformation from the ordinary to the sublime. The thing is, this happens regularly for people from many towns and cities in America, but not many of us get a chance to see such a transformation from beginning to end. You have to be in the right place at the right time. I was.

But I get ahead of myself.

I'll come back to the magic, but first let me begin with a confession: on Saturday night, March 15, 2003, I let go of my adult inhibitions in the midst of 149 teenagers and screamed myself hoarse.

It happened when the chairman of the Heritage Music Festival at Disneyland announced that the top festival award was being presented to "Des Moines Roosevelt High School." I jumped to my feet, pumped my hands in the air, and yelled my fool head off.

I was as caught up in the moment, as excited and exhilarated as those band, orchestra, and chamber choir students who had traveled to Anaheim, California, for four days of fun and festival and who now were taking home the top honors.

Later, I wondered if anyone in our hometown would notice. I wondered if the media would bother with a musical triumph when there's so much to be written and shown about the triumphant world of sports.

I wondered how many people know that there are more kids involved in public school music than in all the sports put together.

And I thought about the proposed cuts in music programs and the havoc that may possibly be released on bands, orchestras, choirs, and choruses as they endure changes in teaching staff, plus diminished resources all around.

I am not attacking the administrators or the school boards. I am painfully aware of their difficult choices, and I know that the country's seeming obsession with science, math, and technology education leaves out a lot of art and music programs.

But believe me, life is about more than science, math, and technology. What students learn from music and art programs can't be taught anywhere else.

As a consultant and author, I worked with companies that constantly stressed "teamwork" and cross-functional projects. I always told these managers to stop using the metaphor of sports teams, with their superstars and bench warmers, and think instead of a band or orchestra in which every single player has an important role, in which the whole truly is greater than the sum of its parts, in which the greatest accomplishment is the ensemble. In an orchestra, people do their parts and work together to create something greater than themselves.

Isn't this what good organizations are about? Isn't this what a democracy is about? Isn't this what strong communities are about?

I think there is no better education for becoming a productive member of society than participation in a musical

People travel to wonder at the height of mountains, at the huge waves of the sea, at the long courses of rivers, at the vast compass of the ocean, at the circular motion of the stars; and they pass by themselves without wondering. . . . Now, let us acknowledge the wonder of our physical incarnation— that we are here, in these particular bodies, at this particular time, in these particular circumstances. May we never take for granted the gift of our individuality.

—Saint Augustine of Hippo (354–430)

ensemble. And believe me, no child is ever left behind in a band or orchestra or chorus.

My son Ronald, who was at the time of the Disneyland music festival a senior at Roosevelt, has autism. He was not the most accomplished musician in the band, but he always gave it his best effort. And the band itself was a defining activity for him. Without band, I can't imagine how his high school experience would have been.

While I think of the band as having put a little magic in Ronald's life, that's not the magic or the mystery I started writing about. Just as the awards ceremony was not the high point of the Anaheim trip.

That came earlier in the day when the symphonic band, chamber orchestra, and chamber choir performed. I know that the teachers and students would describe the experience in their own way, but here's my description: it was an utterly mystical experience.

How else would you explain the transformation of a bunch of typical teenagers into divinely performing musical ensembles? Try to picture busloads of young people looking and acting as young people do, that is, dressed in a strangely conformist style—boys in baggy jeans, the waistline relocated somewhere around the mid- to lower buttocks, girls with low-cut jeans and bare bellies—and talking with one another in a language hardly intelligible to aging adults. (This was before texting.)

Then picture those same kids in tuxedos and long black evening dresses, intensely attentive and concentrating fully on their instruments (or voices) and the directions of the conductor, and producing music of a quality unimaginable from high school musicians back when I was one.

It is a transformation I can only describe as mystical, and it is brought about by two factors: One is the transcendent quality of music that inspires kids to reach beyond themselves in order to perform at their peak level of ability. The other is the teachers. I am so grateful for educators who devote their whole lives to bringing forth exquisite music from young people who initially can't even imagine the possibilities of the beauty they can create together.

I wish you, my readers, could have the experience I had, and if you have the opportunity in your own town, take it. From any viewpoint, I can't imagine school activities that produce more positive, lifelong outcomes than music programs.

In the interest of full disclosure, I played in school bands throughout junior high school (now called middle school), high school, and college. I even got a clarinet scholarship to college, but today's high school clarinetists could cut me to shreds (an old student jazz musician term for giving a superior performance).

The Kindness of Strangers

When my wife and I returned recently from our vacation in beautiful Charleston, South Carolina, and Savannah, Georgia, and told our story to friends, the response was, "You really had the vacation from hell."

Considering the chain of experiences beginning with the first airline flight, that assessment is not inaccurate, but Sally and I can't think of it that way. Yes, there were scary minutes and times of frustration and exasperation as one thing after another seemed to go wrong. But the memory of the difficulty fades. Instead, we think of the abiding reservoir of generosity that seems to reveal itself whenever people realize that their help is truly needed.

I know all the complaints about how angry and hostile we're becoming in America, and having traveled a lot, I've had my share of disappointments with how airline travel has changed from comfortable and pleasant into an impersonal cattle car experience in which we passengers often feel that we're treated more like necessary evils than customers.

But now I put all that aside. Here's the story:

Sally and I departed Des Moines, Iowa, at 6:15 a.m. on a Delta flight to Atlanta. Sally quickly went to sleep and, after a little reading, I did too. The next thing I was conscious of was someone saying, "Are you all right? Are you all right?" I awoke to find a couple of passengers gently shaking Sally, who was only slightly responsive. Her eyes were rolled up, she was sweating and pale, and her skin was clammy.

One of the men who'd been questioning her said, "Let's get her on the floor." It turned out he was a surgeon. Another passenger from about four rows back spoke up and knelt on the floor at Sally's head. She was a registered nurse. The flight attendant appeared with an oxygen mask. Sally's heart rate was slow. The nurse tried unsuccessfully to get her to drink water. Sally vomited instead. Everyone seemed to be trying to help in some way, but I never felt so helpless and scared.

We owe thankfulness to God, not sour faces.

—RUMI (1207–1273)

I stated the obvious. "She seems to be breathing very rapidly."

The nurse looked up, smiled, and said, "It's better than not breathing at all." Reassuring and yet not so reassuring.

The doctor said, "We need to get some fluids into her," and asked the flight attendant for an emergency kit that, I learned later, is to be used only by trained medical personnel. It contained IV equipment. The surgeon inserted the needle, and another passenger volunteered to keep the bag elevated.

The flight attendant and a couple of other passengers kept asking if I was okay. I don't know why. Perhaps I was as pale as Sally.

Meanwhile, the plane began to descend rapidly and the captain announced that we would be landing in Evansville, Indiana. Not exactly in everyone's plans. In fact, later in the hospital, Sally kept saying how sorry she was that the other passengers would miss connections and be late because of her.

The nurse and the surgeon remained in position on their knees during the landing. The man holding the bag kept at it. And speaking as a former Air Force pilot, I can say with assurance that the captain made the smoothest landing I've ever experienced on an airliner.

An ambulance and emergency team met the plane, and Sally and I were hustled off. I kept trying to thank everyone—the surgeon, the nurse, the guy holding the IV bag, the other passengers who expressed their concern, and, of course, the flight attendant. I only hope they heard me.

Sally was semi-conscious, but the emergency team said that all her vital signs were good. We were taken to a room in Deaconess Hospital, where Sally was given tests, including an EKG, and hooked up to monitors and another IV while I filled out paperwork. Everyone at the hospital was patient, friendly, reassuring, and helpful. It was as if they sensed my anxiety and wanted to help me as much as they wanted to help Sally.

When I got to Sally's room, she was still fading in and out of sleep. The nurse said, "Everything looks fine," and told me someone else was on the way to examine her. In walked tall, blonde, blue-eyed Sue Krieg. I know it's a cliché, but she radiated such energy and good will that it was as if the room lit up. Sue was proud of her Indiana German heritage, and watching her during the time we were at the hospital, we understood how she got the nickname "Blitz-Krieg."

We knew she was busy—everyone was—but she was almost casual as she asked about Sally, our family, and our home, and then told us about hers while explaining the diagnosis: syncope, commonly called a fainting spell.

Sally's condition seemed to be a combination of sleep loss, dehydration, and an empty stomach. In other words, it was not a stroke or heart attack or any of those critical conditions we might have feared.

We'd been at the hospital only three hours before Sally was cleared for discharge. Sue bid us such a farewell that it was as if we'd been at some kind of reunion. She suggested that Sally not fly again that day, so I called Hertz, explained the situation, and said we would not be able to pick up the car at our destination and that we needed a car in Evansville and would drive it to Charleston, which was the first city on our vacation itinerary. Erma, the Hertz customer service person, had us on our way within fifteen minutes.

We started the twelve-hour drive, planning to get over halfway before stopping for the night. Our bags, of course, were already in Charleston.

About fifty miles south of Evansville, in a somewhat remote spot as we were entering an interstate highway, the left rear tire blew out. I pulled to the side, turned on the emergency flashers, and called Hertz. They said it would be an hour's wait. It was raining.

After fifteen minutes, a semi pulled in front of us and parked. The driver, smiling and shaking his head at the predicament, yelled, "Do you folks want any help?"

"I appreciate it," I said, "but it's raining pretty hard."

He waved his hand in front of his face as if fanning mosquitoes and said, "I been wet before." Then, looking at the tire, he said, "I can change that tire real fast."

I grew up in the South, and when he pronounced tire "tahr," I knew where he was from.

"We called Hertz and they'll be here after while. No sense in you getting messed up."

"I been messed up before," he insisted. "I do this all the time."

Ignoring the rain, he put on the spare tire and threw the flat into the trunk.

"Man, that thing is ruined. You're gonna have to get a new one, or maybe used."

He then told us that there was a truck stop in the next town and headed for his truck. I knew it was not considered courteous in the South to offer money outright, so, handing him a twenty-dollar bill, I said, "I hope you'll let me buy you some supper."

He smiled and thanked me but refused to take the money. We shook hands and he went on his way. I never got his name.

We made our way to a large truck stop in the next town. They couldn't help me, but a red-haired woman said, "Here, honey, let me make some calls. I'm gonna find somebody to help you."

She found a tire man, but he couldn't help and sent us to Wal-Mart.

We never found out whether they had the right size tire because it would have been a six-hour wait. The man there named another tire store, "Po Boys," just down the road.

They had a used one in the right size, but the young man said, "I don't believe I'd trust this tire to go very far. Why don't you try Rick's?" We went to "Rick's." They didn't have the tire either and suggested Firestone. It was almost 5 p.m., and we were beginning to worry that stores would close for the day. The Firestone dealer didn't have the tire, but he quickly called a dealer in the next town and found the right tire. They promised to hold it, so, following directions, we limped to the next town.

Indeed they had the tire, but we were told by a friendly, professional young man that it would be a two-hour wait. I said to Sally,

"Maybe we should get a motel room, go to bed, pull the covers over our heads, and hope there's no tornado coming through. I think we're snake bit on this trip."

But I decided to tell our sad story to the young man. When he heard what we'd been through, he took the car keys and moved us to the front of the line. Not only that, but he said he frequently visited Charleston and gave us driving directions, even taking time to detail a route around Nashville. "Then," he said, "you'll have some curvy roads when you get to the Smoky Mountains." We were back on the road in thirty minutes.

If the only prayer you said in your whole life was, "thank you," that would suffice.

—MEISTER ECKHART
(1260–1329)

At some point on the long drive, my cell phone rang. It was the Delta airlines station manager back in Evansville calling to check on Sally's condition. "Just wanted to make sure she was all right," he said.

Though it rained all the way, we arrived in Charleston safely. The rain put a damper on the walking we like to do, so we signed up for a guided bus tour. It went well until about halfway through the tour, when the bus broke down. We walked through the rain back to our hotel.

The next day, we drove in the rain to Savannah. Even with all our hardships, Sally and I celebrated with great appreciation the beauty of Charleston and Savannah with their wonderful homes and spectacular dogwoods, azaleas, and wisteria. Happily, we had an uneventful airline trip home.

Back in Des Moines, when friends hear our tale, they say, "You had the vacation from hell." I don't respond, but when I reflect on the trip and on all the people who helped us—the surgeon, the nurse, the flight attendant, other airline passengers, emergency medical workers, nurses, Sue Krieg, the Hertz people, the truck driver, the woman at the truck stop, the Firestone man—I realize that there were just too many angels along the way to think the trip had anything to do with hell.

Moments of Gratitude

Perhaps an Angel

While shopping for groceries, I saw a friend whose husband is suffering with a long-term, debilitating, and ultimately fatal disease. We stood by our grocery carts and hugged for a good long minute.

A woman, a complete stranger to both of us, approached and said, "You both need a hug from me." She then hugged us and began to go on her way. Over her shoulder, she said, "That's what happens when you have love in your heart."

Thinking of Biscuits

It seems more than strange to me that I could have spent my childhood years between the slum streets of Memphis and the piney woods and red dirt hills of Mississippi, now to be sitting in the Jan Tabak Hotel in The Netherlands, drinking chardonnay and eating fish from the North Sea.

I was pulled into this reverie by the little roll they served with unsalted butter that tasted just like one of Aunt Cassie's buttermilk biscuits. Sweet memory.

Poems

Summer

It is early.
I am driving northeast.
The sun skims the soybeans,
    the corn rises from the ground
    like a green wall at the end of the bean field
    at an angle that's right in every way,
    a comfort, an affirmation
    of the dependability of things
    good and growing.

Patience

The porch was alive with hummingbirds,
Swarming the feeders,
Hovering with their invisible wings,
Darting away and back,
Delighting all of us dude ranchers
Sitting in the big Adirondack chairs
After a day on the trail.
Ignoring the admonitions,
Ronald could not stay away.
"Don't worry," the ranch boss said,
"He can't catch them."
But the boss did not count on a patience
He'd never witnessed before:
A boy, moving as slowly as the wings were fast,
The birds waiting to be cupped in the boy's hands,
Then released back to their busy work,
Each christened with a new name.

Section Two
For Family

Does Love Ever Die?

My first wife, the mother of my two older sons, died recently. We divorced more than forty years ago, but I was profoundly grieved by her passing. I was sad, of course, for my sons who had lost their mother, but beyond that, I was sad for myself.

I know there are those who would question my grief over the death of someone from whom I was divorced. The answer, I believe, is found somewhere within the nature of love.

We've all heard the expression, "Love never dies." But is that true? Maybe we should add, "But love changes." I don't mean it changes from one person to another, but it changes in the particular power that gives people the comfort and support and intense connection they need to stay married. Perhaps it's that change that loosens the bonds.

I don't know. I do know that divorce is no less complicated than marriage. It is, at the same time, an ending and a beginning, and having been through it, I can't believe that anybody makes the transition without suffering some sense of loss, regardless of the next phase of their lives.

So back to the question of why I grieved the passing of someone from whom I am divorced. The better question is, how could I not be saddened by the death of someone I loved and with whom I had children, someone who left her last year of college to go with me into the world, someone who'd endured the harrowing experience of being a jet fighter pilot's wife and seeing other young wives become young widows, someone who'd worried and prayed with me when our son was stricken with epilepsy?

Of course I was sad.

This whole process has brought clarity to my feelings about the divorce and has given me perspective. I realize that it's okay for me to look back at the good years and the shared experiences and to be grateful for them without regretting the divorce itself. I do regret what it put my sons through, and that's a pain I simply have to deal with.

Thou has given so much to me. . . . Give me one thing more— a grateful heart.

—GEORGE HERBERT
(1593–1633)

But I am also the most fortunate of men in that my wife of thirty years, Sally, not only understood but also supported me as well as her stepsons. It is she who has arranged the planting of a tree on the state-house grounds to honor the memory of their mother.

When we gather at the planting, I know I'll be sad again, but standing there with my sons and with Sally, I think I'll understand at last the truth that, indeed, "Love never dies."

I'll Read This Again on Mother's Day

I'm sure most of us are grateful for our mothers. If we're not, we should be. Let me tell you about mine and why I am particularly grateful for her life. Were it not for my mother's influence, I would probably have gone to jail at some point.

My father, mother, and I were living a pretty good life in Memphis when my father decided to leave, marry someone else, and make another life, leaving Mother and me on our own and somewhat destitute.*

Mother had studied art at an all-girls' Baptist college in Mississippi, and she was not prepared to support a six-year-old son and herself.

She tried to teach art, but there was no money in it. Soon, a lack of income drove us to move from our nice neighborhood to Lamar Terrace, a federal government housing project that most good citizens called a "slum."

In those days, just as World War II was beginning, Mother went from one job to another, learning lessons she had never dreamed of about life, about power, about class and status, about men who accosted her with no provocation at all—one of them asking her once in front of me and before I knew what it meant if she would like a bedfellow—and about bosses who worked her hard and paid her poorly.

After working in five-and-dime retail sales and briefly on a "war plant" assembly line, she got a job with Memphis Light, Gas, and Water Company, working "in an office," a distinction that seemed to mean a lot to her. A few years later, Mother made a great breakthrough when she studied and learned to use a comptometer machine, which was for its day a super adding machine/calcula-

From David learn to give thanks for every-thing. Every furrow in the book of Psalms is sown with the seeds of thanksgiving.

—Jeremy Taylor (1613–1667)

tor, thus improving her status and her pay. I remember being proud and impressed when, at church, she told people she was a comptometer operator, pronouncing "comptometer" musically as if it were a foreign word.

"What do you do at the Light Company, Ruth?" people would ask, the women being somewhat suspicious of any woman who worked outside the home.

"I'm a comptometer operator," she would answer, her voice rising in the middle of the word, at the "tom" syllable, imbuing it, I'm sure she thought, with special meaning. I think now how pathetic it must have seemed to the church businessmen who knew about such menial things.

Her job was always a struggle, and I saw her fall into tears many a day after returning from her office to our little three-room apartment at 602-J Camilla in Lamar Terrace. It often turned out that the men in the office had "kidded" her. It was a long time before I understood what that meant.

It was all Mother could do to pay the rent, plus buy clothes and school supplies for me, plus dress herself appropriately, plus buy groceries, give her tithe to the church (struggling always with the definition of "tithe"), and come up with eleven cents every Saturday so I could see the double feature matinee at the Linden Circle theatre.

Her greatest goal seemed to be that I grow up to be a "Christian gentleman" and that she be able to hold her head up and look people in the eye and not be ashamed of her life. This meant, I think, that she wanted to move someday from the federal housing project—"just a slum," she also called it—to a house in a nice neighborhood.

Although I don't know for sure, I believe she also thought she might find a good man to marry. She dated a bit, sometimes bringing home a man for me to meet, then strolling with him to the benches on the playground, where occasionally I sneaked into the bushes to watch them kiss.

But it seemed there weren't many good men around. In fact, as I think back on it now, I realize that, in those years during World War II, Mother went out with a series of the sorriest jerks you can imagine.

I used to play the pest so they would bribe me with movie fare to leave them alone. How was I to know they just wanted to get my mother into bed? Did they? I don't know.

I do know about the tears and the depression and the courage and the pride. I do know about bosses who hassled her and married men who told her they were getting a divorce. I know about strangers who propositioned her even as she was walking hand in hand with me along the street. I know about her getting fired because she did not vote the way her supervisor wanted her to vote.

She did marry again, eventually, to a widower with two children. We all moved into his house in a modest neighborhood. As it turned out, he was mean, took Mother's paycheck as his own, and slapped her around a bit when he was irritated. His children did not seem offended; apparently he'd done the same to their mother.

I was scared of him. He was a large, red-haired man who always seemed angry and menacing. When he was unhappy with me, he locked me out of the house for the night. I slept in the park.

Mother filed for divorce after only a year, and at the age of fourteen, I had to testify in court for the first time. I was so nervous I could hardly hear the questions.

The divorce was granted, and once again Mother, a two-time loser in marriage, was challenged to hold up her head among her lady friends in church and at Eastern Star at a time when divorce was not common.

You can imagine how she was treated by men in a series of subsequent jobs.

Throughout these years, she kept me active in Calvary Baptist Church in Memphis, and she drilled me frequently on how a "Christian gentleman" should behave. I was conflicted by this because my Lamar Terrace friends were committing minor acts of vandalism and getting into fistfights. I think now how benign these unlawful acts were compared to what we read about today.

Thanksgiving is good but thanks-living is better.

—Matthew Henry
(1662–1714)

Her devotion to my well-being always seemed to overcome my temptations to, as she put it, "run wild in the streets."

She got a better job finally, and we moved to a more respectable neighborhood, but once again money problems forced us to move and live with my grandmother for a while.

And now the happy ending: Mother's high school teacher, Wilson McKinstry, had never married, and after both of her divorces he had written to offer his support.

She had "gone to school to him," (been his student) as they put it in older days, but she'd hardly seen him since. His letters were friendly and generous in content, and then they became more affectionate. At one point he said he'd been in love with her since her school days, but he did not push her. I think he was an old-fashioned romantic at heart.

Finally, one thing led to another, and the two of them decided to get married. The ceremony was held in my apartment at the university, and afterward we had lunch at a popular student place on the square in Oxford.

She moved with him back to her girlhood home of Blue Mountain, Mississippi, where she became active in the community, took up her painting once again, and became a fairly well-known painter of what we called "Mississippi Primitives."

She and Mr. McKinstry, after twenty years together, died ten days apart. Her obituary ran in *Variety*, citing her as an artist. She must have smiled in her grave.

I don't think I ever truly appreciated what my mother was living through until much later in my life. And I probably never sufficiently expressed it.

But what a story. What a woman. What a mother.

Thanks be to God.

* *Dad did make a good life; he and my stepmother had a good and loving relationship, and after a few years, I began to spend long visits with them and am still close to my half-sister and half-brother. But that's another story.*

A Brother's Testimony

Twenty years ago, my wife and I organized a family picnic with my son Rick, his wife, and their young son. We went to a local park where Ronald, our son with autism who was seven years old at the time and barely verbal, began his usual obsessive routine of throwing sticks into the lake.

He would throw a stick or rock, watch it arc through the air, and then, when it splashed into the water, would clap his hands. At the time, he was also fixed on flags waving. The challenge for us was always trying to break through his obsessions and get his attention.

I did not know that Rick was paying such close attention to Ronald. Months after the picnic, Rick showed me a publication called *Kaleidoscope: International Magazine of Literature, Fine Arts, and Disability.* It contained a commentary and poem he had written, which are reprinted below.

I was almost overwhelmed with gratitude for this evidence of Rick's love for Ronald and for the realization that Rick was trying to understand him and was with us in the struggle.

Visions
By Rick Autry

The poem is about my seven-year-old autistic brother repeatedly throwing sticks in a lake and then clapping as each stick strikes the lake. He quite literally never gets tired of doing this. The form is meant to imitate the theory that autism is partially caused by sensory overload. According to this theory, an inability to filter sensory input and selectively direct focus results in withdrawal in order to avoid complete overload. If this is even a partially accurate explanation, then the consciousness of my brother, I conclude, must differ in significant ways from mine. Thus the title "Visions." (A vision is a refocus of consciousness.)

I had previously considered this issue of "visions" with respect to my own epilepsy. As I have been seizure free for many years now, I have only recollections (albeit vivid ones) concerning my seizures and in any event am as of now unable to capture their mix of loss of control, disembodied peace, and terror. Somehow it was easier to write about Ronald first.

[*This poem is complex and requires concentration to decipher.*]

The Poem
a voice speaks (a flag is flapping) my (sweat rolls down) name (i)
(my face) the breeze (am) i /clap/ is hot (being bitten) in the wind
(my shoes) /clap/ (a stick tumbles and i watch it /clap/ tumble)
smell the (are too big) (into the) scent /clap/ (water) the light
(by a) rolls (i can touch) across a voice of pine
the bark of speaks my stick mosquito /clap/ (name) scratch
throwthe lookwhois stickandwatchthe speakingto /clap/ ittumble
/clap/ /clap/ andmynamescratchthelightrollsfallintotherollsacross
whoispeakingwahcoriosssptehaekwianvge /clap/ andsendoutmyname
/clap/ /clap/ /clap/ /clap/ look who is (i hear clapping) I must
(speaking) watch the (my name) ripples. I must watch the ripples.
/clap/ I must watch the ripples
/clap/I must watch
/clap/ I must /clap/

clap must	clap must
clap must	clap must
clap must	clap must
clap must	clap must

I am ripples.

(November 11, 1991)

Something Like a Resurrection

In January 2009, my wife's parents were in a serious automobile accident.

They were driving home at night after attending a funeral in another town. One of the great road hazards in Iowa during the winter is "black ice," a phenomenon of unexpected glaze ice that can form in nearly invisible patches, especially at night.

My in-laws, Pete and Wineva Pederson, hit the ice, slid backwards across the center line, and slammed into an oncoming car, then were hit by yet another car. The only serious injuries were to Pete and Wineva.

He enjoys much who is thankful for little; a grateful mind is both a great and a happy mind.

—THOMAS SECKER
(1693–1768)

They were rushed to the trauma unit and put in intensive care at the hospital, and the family—three brothers and their wives and two sisters and their husbands (including me)—gathered and, in organized Iowa fashion, decided a schedule to have someone at the hospital twenty-four hours a day.

The future was uncertain. At one point, before Pete was to be taken in for surgery to stop internal bleeding, the doctor came out to the family and said something to the effect that we'd better come say our goodbyes. We gathered around the bed. Pete told us he'd had a good life and if it was time to die, he was ready.

When he was wheeled away, I remember my brother-in-law insisting to the physician that Pete was pretty tough, that he'd gone through

World War II, had stayed active and fit, even trimming trees with a chainsaw and so on. The doctor's response was that Pete had had bypass surgery and some circulation problems and that we shouldn't get our hopes up.

Meanwhile, Wineva, who was also seriously injured, was not aware of Pete's condition. During the surgery, family members spent time with her but did not tell her about the doctors' concerns.

After the surgery, Pete was taken into recovery. All we could do was continue praying and trying to keep up our spirits.

Somewhere in this process, a hospital worker appeared and explained that after the accident, the trauma team had to cut off Pete's clothes, including his blue blazer. She delivered the pieces of the clothes to the family, who recovered the contents of the pockets.

Somehow my wife Sally ended up with two crumpled scraps of paper. She didn't pay attention to them at the time and put them in her purse.

To make this story short, Pete and Wineva recovered fully. In fact, in spring 2010, Pete made a hole in one at his local golf course and was featured in the town newspaper. Wineva is back to walking vigorously every day.

> *Gratitude is the fairest blossom which springs from the soul; and the heart of man knoweth none more fragrant.*
>
> —HOSEA BALLOU
> (1771–1852)

Now to the crumpled scraps of paper. When Sally opened them, she found two prayers (reprinted below). Pete is an elder in his church, and the prayers were ones he used in the serving of Communion, one for the bread and one for the wine. Apparently he'd worn the blazer to church and then later to the funeral without emptying that particular pocket.

Sally kept the papers, not knowing what to do with them until recently when we were getting ready to celebrate Pete's ninetieth birthday with a family gathering. In preparation for the event, Sally straightened the scraps, made copies for the siblings, and had the originals framed under glass. At the birthday celebration, she presented them to her father while recounting the story to the gathered family.

Sally carries her copies of these prayers in her purse as a reminder of God's grace. I suspect her siblings keep them close at hand as well.

The wreck, the struggle, recovery, and the celebration remind us of the gift of life, how it can be taken away in an instant, and why we should pause and be grateful for it every day.

For the bread:

Lord of integrity, remind us that bread ties all of us together, that bread broken your way serves to keep life together, and that bread given in your name speaks meaning and purpose where there is doubt and darkness. Help us to see our lives in the light of broken bread, becoming nourishment to every person we meet.

For the cup:

We rejoice, Father, in your coming to meet us at this table. We are awed at your coming for we do not believe ourselves worthy of your presence. We are afraid of your coming for we are afraid to change our ways on earth. But you come and invite us to drink from the cup of your son, and we thank you.

Moment of Gratitude

Happy Boy

In the early years of our son Ronald's autism, we had many struggles with his behavior. His frustrations often drove him into a tantrum. Any sudden change of activity or location would mean screaming, kicking, biting his hand, and generally getting out of control. He did not respond to firm language or threats. Cajoling and promised rewards did not work either. Many times, Sally and I had to wait him out and learn to ignore the disapproving stares of other parents who must have wondered why we couldn't "control" our child.

Once, during those years when he was perhaps six years old, he came jumping down the stairs one at a time, saying on each stair, "Happy boy, happy boy."

On another day during that same period, he walked into the living room, stopped, spread his arms, and said, "Ta-da!"

I know that seems unremarkable, like pretty normal stuff—which of course is the point.

I still choke up thinking of those moments of gratitude that happened twenty-two years ago.

Poems

Optimism

My grandmother seemed to live through the great depression
and world war two
with an attitude of expectation.
"When my ship comes in," she'd say,
"we'll buy that . . . " (whatever it was),
then go about her work with a cheerfulness
I could never understand.
What was the ship she was expecting,
and where was it coming from?
When I was older I decided she was just trying
to say we didn't have any money.
Later, I came to realize
that it was her way of saying
things will get better.
Later still, I understood
that it was her way to hold on to
the blessing of her eternal optimism.

A Sentimental Poem
For Sally on our 20th Wedding Anniversary

I know that contemporary poets,
if they are to escape the wrath of critics,
must avoid the curse of sentimentality,
but here I am, twenty years married today,
with nothing to write about love
that is not sentimental:
a tumor, a surgery, a scribbled prayer
and the one hundred and thirty-ninth psalm;
the diagnosis of something wrong,
something wrong with our child;
hours and days and years
of working to help him find himself
in this world;
deaths of a father, a brother, a beloved sister,
more surgeries and recoveries,
a son in the struggle with addiction.
And I haven't even gotten to the joys,
not talked about the celebrations of life,
the friendships, the gatherings of family,
and the great and enduring spiritual quest.
If I am doomed to write of sentiment,
then let it be said that I also write of blessing,
all of it, the pain, fear, anguish,
laughter, whimsy, joy, blessings all,
because you arrived in my life
with an expectation of blessing,
a sure belief that there is nothing but abundance
and our job is to face it all with gratitude.

Section Three
For Friends

Tribute to Old Friends

I am blessed with many friends. I don't mean social acquaintances or former workplace colleagues; I mean dear, close friends. I'd like to tell you about all of them and try to demonstrate how special they are, but that would take up more pages than I have, and I suspect you'd get bored pretty fast.

But I do want to write about my two oldest male friends. By that I mean friendships from sixty years ago for which I'm thankful every day.

I am in touch with these men regularly, both fellow graduates from the University of Mississippi. The two are different in many ways, but we are connected through music, aviation, and philosophy. We don't frequently see one another face to face, but phone calls and e-mail help us stay current. Just writing about them for this book makes me feel close to them once again.

Sam Gore is the adventurer. He's appropriately cautious but far less cautious than I am; I often say he'll try anything that's legal and does-

In the deepest night of trouble and sorrow God gives us so much to be thankful for that we need never cease our singing. With all our wisdom and foresight we can take a lesson in gladness and gratitude from the happy bird that sings all night, as if the day were not long enough to tell its joy.

—SAMUEL TAYLOR COLERIDGE
(1772–1834)

n't cost too much. He and I were in ROTC together in college, went through pilot training, and then served together in France as Air Force jet fighter pilots during the Cold War.

I left the Air Force to pursue my journalism career, but Sam stayed in, later flying combat missions in Vietnam and being awarded the Distinguished Flying Cross. He left the Air Force, bought some land in his home county in Mississippi, and went to work for Eastern Air Lines.

For most former Air Force pilots, that would seem like a stable, long-term career, but the man who owned Eastern managed to strip it of assets and take it into bankruptcy, leaving Sam without most of his pension.

He went to crop-dusting school (one of aviation's riskiest professions), and later began flying bush in Alaska, hauling salmon in an often maximum-loaded single-engine plane from the fishermen to the processing plants. He finally set up his own fishing operation but still continued flying for others. That kind of flying is probably more hazardous than crop-dusting.

He stopped in Iowa on several occasions en route from Mississippi to Alaska, his plane with its big tundra tires creating a bit of a stir among the slick private jets at the Des Moines airport.

He's done with all that now and settled in Mississippi, where he puts a great deal of energy and effort into playing music. For several years, he and I and some friends played together in a group we called the "Over the Hill Jazz Band." Sam continues to play in venues around north Mississippi as well as on jazz cruises. Just as he is a better pilot than I am, he's a better musician than I am, a fact I enjoy rather than envy.

Once or twice a year we share an adventure on the Mississippi River south of Memphis. To be on that river is unlike any other water experience.

The way you perceive the river is how it is. If you see it as menacing, it definitely can be that. If you see it as glistening and fresh, it can be that as well. The river has personality. It's unpredictable, smooth one minute seeming to guide you along, then filled with whirlpools and undertow, carrying you where it wants you to go.

Sam and I set forth in a thoroughly disreputable van, pulling an only slightly less disreputable boat named *The Death Wish II* (in honor of the first boat, which leaked) and put out perhaps a hundred hooks. We then head to a motel where we eat barbecue and drink beer; the next morning we get on the river early and pull in our fish. We never fail to catch a lot of big catfish.

I confess it is a "roots" experience, inextricably entwined with our history, our heritage, and our friendship. How could I not be deeply grateful?

Jim Ferguson is the consummate teacher, and I have learned much from him.

We played in the marching and concert bands in college. Jim majored in music, later getting his doctorate in music education. For years he was a high school band director and was then chosen as band director at our alma mater. Later he became band director of the University of Alabama's famed "million dollar band."

It always seemed to me that he was able to create a mystical connection with the band members that inspired them to perform well beyond what they thought they could. He once wrote me that, "as with all art, one hopes that the effect or outcome will be an enhanced sense of connection, a oneness, a feeling of belonging and understanding. . . . The 'bird of spirituality' will have, to some degree, made itself known to the listener."

It's difficult to give you real insight into the way Jim's musical mind works and why I delight in our conversations and his e-mails, so let me share the e-mail he sent after a fishing trip:

> Just got back from a two-day fishing trip with Jimmy [Jim's son] and some of his friends. I thought of you as we were motoring along in a large outboard rig. I was harmonizing with the harmonic series of the outboard motor and just slipped off into Shostakovich's fifth. Knew you would be the only one I knew who would find that sort of interesting.
>
> As I was singing the 3rd, 5th, and 9th harmonics (no 7th audible), it occurred to me that the motor was outlining the history of

music. Octaves and parallel organum of the Notre Dame School (10th century—the 3rd harmonic which is like the fifth of a major chord), the functional 5th harmonic (14th century, Josquin Dupres and others—like the third of a major chord and actually completing the conscious use of the major triad.).

Then the 9th harmonic which functions like the ninth in a major ninth chord (19th century—many composers). For some reason, perhaps where I was sitting in the boat, the 7th harmonic was missing, but I have heard it on most other outboards. (Maybe it needed a tune up. Just kidding). The 8th, 10th, 12th were also present but since they were multiples of the others, not too interesting.

After some consideration and a bit of boredom, I decided to mention it to two of my fellow fishermen, Matt's father and the Cajun guide. I said, "Well, you guys might think I'm crazy for mentioning this to you, but the sounds that outboard motor is making is outlining the history of music."

I didn't have to go any further. The expressions on their faces tipped me off that they agreed that I was crazy, so I dropped the subject. My son Jimmy brought it up tonight. He asked, "Dad, what were you talking about when you told Mr. Steve about the music history thing?"

I heard Jim's bands many times and visited while he was rehearsing the groups. I traveled to the Sugar Bowl game one year just to see his band in action.

When my father died, I called Jim with the news. He cried a bit and said a few words. Several days passed and I received an audiotape in the mail. In Ferguson's way—which is to waste few words—there was no accompanying message. When I played the tape, I realized no message was necessary.

I later learned that, a day or so after my phone call, Jim had interrupted the band's rehearsal for a football game halftime show and passed out some music. He then told his students, "This is

Courtesies of a small and trivial character are the ones which strike deepest in the grateful and appreciating heart.

—HENRY CLAY (1777–1852)

very important to me and we don't have much time, so let's do this the first time through."

I still have the audiotape of the University of Alabama band playing "Amazing Grace," Jim's way of expressing his love and sympathy. In further tribute he had his band perform "Amazing Grace" during halftime at the Cotton Bowl in Dallas, bringing 80,000 cheering people to their feet.

I ask again, as I did about Sam, how could I not be deeply grateful for this friendship?

Friendship and the Blessing of Butterflies

My late friend, Don Mitchell, was a brilliant newspaperman and writer, a speechwriter for a state governor, a staff member with the World Health Organization in Geneva, and, for most of his adult life, a serious alcoholic.

I never understood by what energy and unflagging creative spirit he was able to function for so many years while drunk. And I was amazed by his ability to camouflage his inebriation; I could rarely tell whether he was drunk or sober.

I, among other friends, encouraged him to write, and he'd occasionally turn out a short story, an op-ed piece, or a satirical commentary on the world and its foibles. He was good, but something inside him could not accept success. When things started looking up, he'd fall into alcohol again.

At some point, perhaps twenty-five years after we became friends, he got seriously involved in Alcoholics Anonymous and quietly became sober. He took at job with the Small Business Administration in California, working with minority contractors for the government. Though the job did not involve writing, something about it engaged him in such a way that he found meaning and purpose in it. In addition, he began to mentor and sponsor other people struggling with addiction.

As for writing, he put that energy into letters to friends, much to our great benefit over the years.

Also, to my surprise, he began volunteer work as someone who goes into the field in various seasons and participates in "butterfly counts." This led him to a serious interest in butterflies and their welfare. He worked to establish butterfly habitats in state parks and supported conservation efforts involving banning certain pesticides.

Once, while visiting me in Iowa, he explained that Monarch butterflies require milkweed for reproduction and survival, and he lamented that so many weed control efforts by farmers and state highway departments were diminishing this critical habitat for Monarchs.

At the time, my cocker spaniel had just died. I told Mitch that I did not plan to get another dog and thought I would take down the fence and turn the dog run into some kind of garden.

I awoke this morning with devout thanksgiving for my friends, the old and the new.

—RALPH WALDO EMERSON (1803–1882)

"A butterfly garden," he said, and told me how I should do it and what I should plant. We drove along country roads and harvested milkweed seeds, then chose favorite perennials that attract butterflies, like butterfly bush and butterfly weed (that's what I call them).

That was several years ago. Since then, Mitch has died of cancer. Friends held a memorial gathering at our home at which we recalled his wit, read his writing, and told stories. It was a bittersweet event because we all knew what he'd gone through, and most of us had been with him for part of the journey. His AA group in California produced a CD of photographs. On the cover? A butterfly, of course.

I confess that what I call my "Mitchell commemorative butterfly garden" now looks a lot like a weed patch—overgrown, not manicured, and certainly not what the typical city homeowner would consider attractive landscaping. But I decided that the butterflies like it that way.

And I know Mitchell likes it.

Every year when the butterflies pass through and I walk among the Monarchs and Yellow Swallowtails and watch them flutter up and down into the garden again, I think of Mitchell and how he emerged from the darkness of his addiction into the light of appreciation for his life. I think of how he helped others.

And I say, "Thank you for this gift, Mitch."

Moment of Gratitude

Thank You Every Day

I received a note recently from my friend Perry Snyder. In it, he explained that he was writing a thank-you note to a different friend or colleague every day for a year, 365 notes. What a good idea.

The note is personal, but it concludes with this: "Most of all . . . thank you for your friendship."

This note is a gift I will treasure.

Poem

Fellow Travelers

A boy stutters to me,
his eyes askew behind thick glasses,
about airplanes and coming home from Florida,
about the weather and cars
and anything else that crosses his mind
in these few minutes,
and I recognize him instantaneously,
and want to rush to his parents
and take their hands and,
through the distress and fatigue
they feel changing planes at O'Hare
with this strange and unpredictable child,
cry Yes Yes I know I know
and Don't despair
and We're all in this together
and Despite everything,
it's worth it.

Section Four
For Matters of the Spirit

Unexpected Gifts

After thirty-two years in corporate life and twenty years as an author and consultant, I have served on enough committees and attended enough meetings to last the rest of my life. So my general response to such "opportunities" these days has been to say no, it's someone else's turn, some younger person needs the experience.

But a few months ago, I was taught not only what an awful attitude I had but that sometimes our unwillingness to be inconvenienced can undermine our possibilities for deep human connection and profound spiritual growth.

It began about a year ago when the senior pastor of my church contacted me about serving on a "discernment" committee whose job was to ascertain the qualifications for ordination of one of our ministers who had served as a licensed minister, then to make a recommendation for the next step in the process.

Gratitude is the fairest blossom which springs from the soul.

—Henry Ward Beecher (1813–1887)

I grew up in Southern Baptist churches in the South where sun-reddened young men who felt the call left the cotton fields and became ordained, a process that consisted mainly of the church deacons laying their hands on bowed heads. These young men probably could not have spelled "eschatology," but they read and studied the Bible, and when they felt they could make some everyday sense out of the Scriptures, they began to preach.

I probably would have responded to my senior minister with my usual "no" aside from two reasons: he told me that the candidate for ordination had specifically asked that I serve on the committee, and the candidate had become a friend and had been the indispensable influence in helping my son with autism become a full participant in the community of worship. I felt I owed her much more than service on a committee.

Besides, I figured it would be self-evident that she should be ordained. She worked hard. She studied and attended classes. And she had brought energy, enthusiasm, and a bias toward innovation to her ministerial activities. It seemed like a slam-dunk to me.

I was drawn to my present denomination partly because of its attention to biblical scholarship and its emphasis on an educated clergy. I would soon add to that a commitment to processes of prayerful deliberation in its important decisions. I quickly learned that the journey to ordination, including the discernment committee's work, does not yield to foregone conclusions.

"Slam-dunk" is not in the vocabulary.

Little did I know that in this, as in many experiences, I was to receive far more than I was to give. The first gift was getting to know and work with fellow church members whom I'd seen only at worship. Next was what I learned by working with these extraordinarily accomplished and qualified people.

Having not been raised in a United Churches of Christ (UCC) congregation, I confess that I was relatively ignorant of its history. I did not know, for instance, how much emphasis is put on its ministers having seminary degrees. I knew that the ministers of my acquaintance and certainly the ones serving our church demonstrated considerable theological sophistication, but that was the extent of my knowledge. And to be honest, I didn't much care beyond that. Another awful attitude.

My service on the discernment committee required me to become more knowledgeable about my own church (another gift) because it was revealed that our group would venture into relatively new territory by recommending ordination for a person who did not have the requisite formal seminary education. This was by no means like any other committee experience I'd had, and I hope not to sound overly dramatic, but the process could have had a profound effect on the UCC.

The process involved written papers, discussion, interviews, and much prayerful deliberation. I was greatly impressed by the commitment, hard work, and passion of my fellow committee members, all of whom knew far more about the UCC and the process than I did. Our wise senior minister guided us, but his guidance was informative rather than directive.

After months of work, the committee voted to recommend ordination.

There were more stairs for our candidate to climb, but we on the committee knew that our recommendation was key.

As the date of the ordination ceremony drew near, I was honored to be asked to represent the committee and the congregation. Each participant had a part to play, and at the end, after the voting, there came the familiar laying on of hands. I was honored to be part of that as well.

Then came a moment of gratitude I shall never forget. As the about-to-be-ordained minister knelt, I could sense the enormous wave of emotion surging through her. She could not contain her tears, and I was having trouble containing my own. For a reason I cannot explain, I put my hand on her cheek. I had a brief fear of having violated some ceremonial protocol, but she then put her hand on my hand, and we held hands while she knelt.

I know the idea of "feeling at one" with someone, something, the universe, or God is probably greatly overused, but I can't find a better description of how I felt. Here comes another overused word: "transcendent." That too is how I felt, that the human exchange in that moment during the ceremony transcended the merely human and somehow connected the divine within both of us—the greatest gift of all.

An Invocation

Sometimes it's difficult to know how to pray. I know what I'm supposed to do: "Just pray from the heart"; "Open up and let it flow"; and so on. And I know what I'm not supposed to do: "Don't write it down"; "Don't make a sermon out of it."

Still, with all the well-meaning advice, I know a public prayer can send unappreciated messages if I'm not careful. For instance, I was asked to give an invocation a few years ago at a dinner for leaders in the natural products business, a highly diverse group of people from diverse faith traditions and with highly diverse beliefs. I wanted to be sensitive to those folks while also not abandoning my faith and what it says about prayer. I wanted to try to add helpful thoughts about our purpose in coming together in the first place.

Gratitude is born in hearts that take time to count up past mercies. They are the charming gardeners who make our souls blossom.

—CHARLES EDWARD JEFFERSON (1860–1937)

Yes, I wrote it down. Here it is:

We don't know who you are, God, Goddess, Lord, Spirit, Creator. All we know is that you are known by many names and in many forms. Yet we feel and experience your essence through the love and grace and blessing in our lives. We have already felt your presence in this gathering, and we ask that you be in and around and among and within us these days as we go about our deliberations and as we find pleasure in one another's company.

We come here seeking wisdom. We want answers; we want to know what to do and how to do it, both in our business enterprises and in our lives. And yet, we already know that the path will never be easy to see or simple to follow, so help us find the presence to be in the moment, every moment, every day, to cast off the fears and anxieties that plague us and prevent us from becoming the best people we can be in every circumstance.

Help us to live life with gratitude for what we have, for what we've done, for what we are trying to do, and for how we are trying to be. In simpler words, help us to count our blessings.

Now, remembering the admonition of Meister Eckhardt that, in prayer, it is enough to just say thank you, let all the people here, all together, just say "Thank you."

Thank you. Amen

And, I am happy to report, all those businesspeople said, "Thank you."

The Unending Quest for Understanding

My late brother once told me that he considered biblical scholarship to be an act of worship, and then he quoted from Pastor John Robinson's farewell speech to the Pilgrims: "I am verily persuaded the Lord hath more truth and light yet to break forth from his holy word."

I don't think I understood what my brother was getting at. After all, I thought in those days, the Bible has been around for a long time, and surely we know what it says. And how, I wondered, could someone spend his or her entire life worrying about every word in the Bible to figure out what it says?

That was an ignorant and limited attitude; more than that, it was a sign of my laziness in not being willing to think beyond the obvious. Much later I learned, partly from my own experience as a writer and poet, that more often than not, what lies underneath the words is most important. Put another way, the deeper meaning may be revealed only through reading and rereading, carefully exploring each word and phrase for what the writer is trying to say.

And of course, many writings, including the Scriptures, operate on several levels. The parables, for instance, can be understood as fairly simple stories, but research into the cultural, historical, and religious context of those stories can reveal more complex and textured levels of meaning and provide us with a richer experience and understanding.

I now realize how right my brother was. We need theologians and scholars who dedicate their lives to the great quest for truth and understanding, and I am grateful for them. Our faith and our world benefit from their work (or, as my brother would put it, from their "acts of worship").

Moment of Gratitude

Old Hymns

I have belonged to what is called a mainline progressive Protestant church, Plymouth Congregational United Church of Christ, for over twenty years. I like everything about it—the emphasis on the two commandments to love God and to love our neighbor and the activism on behalf of justice. But I confess there have been times I've missed the old hymns. I grew up singing shaped note gospel from the old Stamps-Baxter hymnals. And deeply embedded in my memory are images of my mother doing housework and singing "Have Thine Own Way, Lord" and "In the Garden."

About two years ago, the wife of one of our pastors who is herself an ordained minister took over the band at the Saturday evening family service. She is a wonderful musician: singer, guitarist, banjo player, and, as we'd say in the South, I don't know what-all else.

She is from Alabama.

I probably don't have to tell you what changes she brought to the music; I'll just say that sometimes I find myself singing hymns like "I'll Fly Away" and thinking of the old-time revival meetings of my youth.

Poems

New Birth
For Sally, Spring 1984

From her sure knowledge
that everything would come out all right,
things began to come out all right,
out through the present day horrors,
through my fears and loss and grief,
through the demons lurking around everything I do.
As if directly from that optimism,
Ronald came unconcerned into the cold and light,
no longer surrounded by the sounds of Sally's life,
but sliding easily into the doctor's bloody hands
then snuggling back onto his mother's warmth,
none of his father's wailing against the world,
none of that waiting for the next shoe to fall.
And I count toes and fingers
and check his little penis
and touch the soft spot on his head
and watch the doctor probe and squeeze,
not believing that everything came out all right.

Later I wonder how these years have come
from pain to death to pain to life
to what next?
A baby babbling in the backpack,
a mother walking her healthy pace,
a dog trailing behind,
and me holding on,
through the neighborhood, through everything,
with each day
one by one
coming out all right.

From Life after Mississippi, 1989

Every Day a Blessing
For Sally on our 20th wedding anniversary

You have a way
of turning everything into a blessing,
of seeing the great mystery of goodness
in whatever happens,
in wherever we find ourselves in this life.

Waiting for the surgeons to cut your throat
you shared the 139th Psalm,
more to comfort me than you,
and somehow the surgery turned into
a celebration of life.

When they said something was wrong with our child,
and I sank into despair,
you learned what to do and how to do it,
showed the joy in every little triumph
from sign language to potty training,
and taught me the power of gratitude.

I've been told there is a light to guide us,
so bright it cannot be seen with the eyes,
that if we are to see it at all
we must find it inside ourselves.
Through all the fear and disappointment
and even through the loss of beloved people,
you have been able to live in that light,
and in turn have become the light
that I can see and follow,
the blessing of my life,
blessing upon blessing upon blessing.

Section Five

For Those Who Serve

For Those Who Deserve
Our Gratitude

When I was a kid during World War II, I desperately wanted the war to last long enough for me to get into it. That was childish exuberance, of course, but in my teenage years and into college it never occurred to me that I would not serve in the military, either as a volunteer or as a draftee.

Now young people no longer have the draft and its possibilities hanging over their heads and no longer serve in the military unless they volunteer. Personally, I don't think that's a good thing, but my purpose here is not to defend the draft. I leave that to others.

Gratitude is happiness doubled by wonder.

—G. K.
CHESTERTON
(1874–1936)

I want to emphasize the effect that World War II had on so many of us, particularly boys—how we followed the news, how we learned about the weaponry and the military terminology, how we were mesmerized by the movies of the day. The war was glorified and made attractive to us.

Meanwhile, older boys, some only a few years older than we, were actually fighting that war. They have been called the "greatest generation" and have been honored in many ways during the past decade. Still, I am amazed that so many people know so little about those years and that war; I'm more amazed that so many people don't seem to care, preoccupied I guess with their daily lives.

And it's true that we can't live in the past, but we also must honor the past. These thoughts came to mind recently when I read an obituary about a ninety-year-old businessman. It contained this sentence somewhat buried in the middle of a paragraph: "(He) . . . served in the 8th Air Force 392 Bomb Group in the European Theater of Operation as a radio operator/advanced bombardier and was a member of The Caterpillar Club."

I couldn't help thinking that a whole history was contained in that one sentence, a story of fear and the constant threat of death. That sentence could have been translated simply, "He had to go through hell on a regular basis."

Being a "radio operator/advanced bombardier" meant sitting for hours in an airplane loaded with bombs, being harassed and shot at by enemy fighters, dodging flak, watching sister airplanes go down and counting the parachutes to see how many crewmen got out.

Being a "member of The Caterpillar Club" meant that you also had to "bail out," to use the parachute to survive. It meant you had to "hit the silk." Parachutes were made from silk at the time, so the connection of silk to caterpillars led to the name of the club. Anyone who had to bail out was a member. The term was still in use when I was an Air Force pilot, even though parachutes had long since been made from other materials.

It would be easy to skip over this little part of the obituary, and I guess I should not be surprised that it did not mean much to many people. But it should mean a lot to all of us.

Once, during the Battle of Britain, Winston Churchill asked an R.A.F. bomber pilot to describe flying. He replied that it consisted of hours and hours of boredom punctuated by moments of stark terror.

Stark terror. Consider that for a moment.

I am grateful for the service of that businessman who came home, held a good job, got married, had children, played golf, was a Mason and a Shriner, and "had a great sense of humor."

Not long after seeing his obituary I happened to watch the movie *Memphis Belle* about a B-17 crew in the 8th Air Force during World War II. At the end of the film, there was a note that 200,000 air crew members were killed over Europe during that time.

To Serve and Protect

It seems we're always reading stories in the big-city newspapers about police corruption or police brutality. I know this goes on, and we even have cases of it in good old Des Moines, but I am persuaded that these are the exceptions. So I want to offer another perspective.

Full disclosure: I've rarely been stopped for speeding and have never been arrested, thus I don't have much experience on the receiving end of police action.

Nonetheless, even without that, I know this: Law enforcement officers work hard, have a difficult and dangerous job, are underpaid, and rarely get thanked for their service.

When we think of police officers, I suspect that not many of us are aware of the variety of situations they face and how perceptive, flexible, and, yes, sensitive they must be. They may go from traffic stops to serious accidents to dealing with public intoxication to armed robberies to helping elderly people who have wandered from home to domestic violence to high-speed chases—and they might face more than one of those on any given day.

And those different situations and different people have to be dealt with in different ways. Consider this: An officer is called to a business establishment because a patron is behaving irrationally and won't leave. On arriving, the officer has to determine first if the person is a danger to himself or others. Is he armed? Is he drunk? Is he on drugs? And this analysis has to be done quickly and under much pressure. At the same time, the person's rights must be respected. It is a challenge to say the least.

In those situations, the officer may also face a person with an intellectual or mental disability. We can't expect the police to be psychologists or behavioral therapists, but they must have a basic understanding and some techniques for recognizing and solving the problems without force or an arrest, which would only escalate and exacerbate the situation.

Last year, our progressive chief of police determined that it would help everyone if the police could have training in recognizing the behaviors and symptoms of people with these conditions. As part of the chief's initiative, she asked my wife and me, who are advocates of many years for disability rights, to participate in the production of a training video. I have heard that it was well received by the officers and has been a great help to them. This gives comfort to parents and loved ones of people with disabilities who are always vulnerable to misunderstanding and misinterpretation of their behaviors.

I'm grateful in many ways for our law enforcement professionals. Like politicians, they often get a bum rap.

I'm a veteran, and it's not unusual for people, particularly people of a certain age, to say, "Thank you for your service." I'm thinking how good it would be if, when we had the chance, we told a police officer, "Thank you for your service." He or she would appreciate it more than we can imagine.

Gratitude for (Gasp!) Politicians

Politicians are an easy target these days.

It is rare that a person will say one good word about politicians. But try this experiment: Rather than asking someone about "politicians," ask instead about their particular congressperson or senator or city council member or school board member.

I suspect you'll find sort of an "I'm okay, you're not okay" response. Most people tend to condemn politicians generally but feel that their own representatives do a pretty good job.

That's a generalization, of course, but if you exclude the habitually angry folks who blame all politicians for our problems, I think you'll find that, like many generalizations, it's true.

Let me be clear: I disagree with the policy positions of a lot of politicians, and I would not vote for them, but I know this: they are not villains. They are, for the most part, honest, hard-working people who are trying to do the right thing for their constituents and for their state and country. They are bombarded with letters, emails, phone calls, and visitors. They put in unbelievable hours and are on call virtually twenty-four hours a day, every day, wherever they are.

Are some of them crooks and charlatans and fools? Of course, but in my experience in business, nonprofit work, and education, I must say that the field of politics does not have an exclusive claim on crooks and charlatans and

The hardest arithmetic to master is that which enables us to count our blessings.

—Eric Hoffer (1902–1983)

fools. And unlike business "leaders," public office holders are accountable directly to the people every two or four or six years. We can vote them out.

I agree that money in politics has gotten out of hand and that elected officials have to devote an inordinate amount of time to, as my congressman calls it, "dialing for dollars." But the problem is not that they have to raise money; it's that campaigns cost so much money in the first place. And while I agree that campaign contributions can "buy" access—that is, the contributor is often able to make his or her case directly to the candidate or incumbent—I also know this: the politicians have to satisfy the people who vote with their ballots not with their dollars. It is rare that a politician believes that he or she only has to satisfy the contributors instead of the voters.

Also, in my experience, the average citizen can be heard. Most politicians have people dedicated to "constituent services." They answer letters, respond to phone calls and emails, and try to keep their bosses in touch. It's not an easy job, but they do it.

When I was president of a charitable nonprofit, I did not have money for campaign contributions—it would have been against the law, anyway—but I was able to sit down with senators and congresspeople and lobby directly for legislation that would help our cause.

I want to be clear. I'm no Pollyanna and I'm no fool. I know about the cynicism, the maneuvering, and the deal making, but I know that, like it or not, this is the way our democracy works.

As is so often said, it's not a perfect system, but it's the best system in the world, and I for one am grateful for the people who are willing to get into the arena and try to make it work. It's a difficult job. I hear a lot of people gripe about the politicians, but I don't hear a lot of those gripers volunteering to change places with them.

In closing, a point of disclosure: my wife was lieutenant governor of Iowa for eight years and is still active in public policy. So I've seen a lot of politicians close up, and I think I know what I'm talking about.

Moments of Gratitude

Unsung Hero

Thinking that I was getting some kind of fundraising call, I answered the phone recently with an impatient voice.

"Mr. Autry?"

"Yes, what is it?"

"This is Toad."

Toad, a name that in our family is almost mythical, a name from years past.

I encountered Toad twenty-four years ago when, home from work one day, I met the yellow school bus bringing my then three-year-old son from a public school special class for children with autism.

The bus door opened, and the driver said, "Okay, Ronald, look at me. Look at me."

Ronald looked at the driver.

"Bye, bye, Ronald. Now say 'bye bye.'"

Ronald was not yet verbal, but he tried: "Buhbuh."

"And Ronald?" the bus driver continued. Ronald looked at him.

"Toad loves you, Ronald."

That's how I met Toad, a big happy man who drove kids with intellectual disabilities to and from school. All this was running through my head as I heard his name on the phone.

"Toad," I said. "So good to hear from you. Tell me what you've been up to."

He explained that he was retired and was calling to touch base with some of the kids he remembered.

I told him how grateful we'd always been that he went beyond driving the bus to engage the kids and encourage them to make eye contact and talk, both often difficult for people with autism. I brought him up to date on Ronald and asked him to stop by some time.

"How is retirement?" I asked.

"It's okay, but I miss the kids. Driving and watching out for those kids was the greatest privilege of my life."

Think of that. The greatest privilege of his life! Think of how many people would be bored or discontent in that job, but this big man took time every day to say, "Toad loves you, Ronald."

And we love Toad.

Bread upon the Waters

Several years ago, I decided to retire early from my position as a senior corporate executive and plunge into a new career after thirty-two years. Of all the expressions of congratulations and support, the most moving were from employees and former employees.

Most frequently, they cited something such as a note or letter I had written to them, perhaps years before, expressing sympathy or congratulations. I know that, at the time, those little acts of caring and paying attention had been part of my everyday office activities, sandwiched in among a jillion other things.

Yet, as I read those outpourings of remembrance and affection and good wishes, I began to understand the full meaning of "bread upon the waters" and how our caring returns to us manyfold.

Poem

Debts and Payments

World War II was mostly movies to me,
certainly not headlines,
because I did not read the papers then.
Even the war news came as newsreels
between the features and the cartoons
at the Saturday matinee
so the planes and tanks and soldiers
all were bigger than life,
heroic beyond my imagination,
and we would rush home and play war,
contorting our faces in agony
but always managing to toss one last grenade,
littering our playground with dead Nazis and Japs.

I prayed that the war last long enough
for me to get into it
but it was not to be.
The soldiers returned with medals and money and war brides.
And stories.
Slowly we learned that the storytellers
had not seen much combat
and that the quiet ones had the real stories
but they were not telling.

Adapted from *Life & Work*

Section Six
For the Pain of Life

Gratitude and Grief

I've always thought there must be a poem in the greetings of a scattered family as they gather at a funeral: embraces awkward and A-frame; back pats and rubs signaling intimacy but not too much; kisses sometimes lingering and sometimes left in the air. And there is always the uncertainty about smiling at a time like this, grimacing instead, saving the real smiles for the wake with its funny remembrances.

There is no substitute for these rituals, as depressing as they can be but as necessary as they are to our well-being and our understanding that every one of us must make this passage sooner or later.

How do we find gratitude in the death of a friend or loved one? The institutional response, of course, is a ceremony often called a "celebration of the life of _____." That's important, and I recall with gratitude the services celebrating the lives of my loved ones. In fact, until I experienced it, I had no idea how important and how comforting the notes and flowers could be.

But don't we also have to go through something more personal, more inside ourselves, in order to move through grief to gratitude? Don't we have to find a redeeming spiritual lesson in our sense of loss? I think so.

In our society, we get conditioned to overcome or, to put it another way, to conquer our grief as if it were an enemy. We're encouraged to leave our grief behind us and "get on" with our lives as if our grief, our loss, is not now an inextricable part of our lives.

We can never leave our grief behind us, and we shouldn't try. We will always feel the absence of a loved one, and the point is not to beat it, not to forget it, not to diminish it in any way; rather, we should transform it into a means of spiritual growth through the great gift of memory and through the realization that there is a presence within absence.

What do I mean by that? Just this: we carry some part of our loved ones with us always, and we can develop ways to feel them with us. My late beloved sister-in-law Susie took great joy in watching birds, and now when a new bird shows up at the backyard feeder, I feel Susie's presence just knowing how much she would have enjoyed identifying it and telling me about it.

As a southerner, I come from storytelling people, and those people have taught me how to feel a lost loved one's presence and how to move from grief to gratitude. They would never have put it that way—it would have sounded too "highfalutin'"—but in telling their stories, their recollections of people now gone, they have kept those loved ones with us. I think of every story as a little resurrection.

Of course it can be painful to remember people and to know we'll never see them again in this life, but in our loss, we can also be grateful for the time our loved ones were present in our lives, and we can learn to open ourselves to all the ways we can feel their presence still: stories, songs, gatherings, worship, and of course, laughter. We can let our memory become a means to transform grief and to create for us a sanctuary of gratitude.

Facing Death with Gratitude

"All of my future days will be counted from this one."

Thus began my late brother Ronald's journal on December 16, 1981, after being told the day before that the bone marrow cancer he'd successfully fought for two years had turned into an aggressive leukemia and that his chances to beat it were slim. He kept the journal for thirty-eight straight days; the entries stopped eighteen days before he died on February 10, 1982, at age sixty.

I retrieved his journal from my file of family memorabilia after I began pondering the subject of facing death with gratitude as part of this book. I didn't know where to begin but thought perhaps Ronald's writings might give me a starting point.

They have given me much more. In fact, they are almost a complete testament to the power of gratitude in the face of anything. I know that I will turn to his writings again and again.

Most of us have had a loved one who faced a dire diagnosis. Perhaps some of you live now with such a diagnosis. It would be foolish, not to mention arrogant, for me to try to tell anyone how to face such news with gratitude.

In ordinary life we hardly realize that we receive a great deal more than we give, and that it is only with gratitude that life becomes rich. It is very easy to overestimate the importance of our own achievements in comparison with what we owe others.

—DIETRICH BONHOEFFER
(1906–1945)

No one's initial response to the probability of suffering and death is to express gratitude, though we know that all of us will die.

I don't suggest that my brother was grateful for his death to come, but he did not let his knowledge of imminent death drive him into despair and self-pity. Rather, that knowledge seemed to inspire within him insights and understandings that reveal a deep appreciation of and gratitude for his life and those in it.

His journal contains lessons for all of us, and part of me wants to have you read all sixty-three pages of it, but there's too much "inside" information and too many personal references that would not mean anything to you. So I have extracted the passages that I think will have the most meaning and will be most helpful to you and those you love.

Rather than follow the journal chronologically, I have arbitrarily organized the passages into categories: faith, marriage, family, friends, and work, plus a few general observations made to himself about his illness.

Faith

References to Ronald's faith run throughout his journal. Here are two, the first of which was written right after the diagnosis:

> So there it is, Self. How do you feel about it?
>
> I don't like it one damned bit, and I'm not going to lie down and take it. But, oh, Creator, you know I mean it when I say your will be done; give me courage and accept my thanks for the years since myeloma and since heart surgery and for all the new starts, for all the things that go with being alive. Self, Self, do you really mean it? I do. . . .
>
> I want intensely to live but one of my offerings to the Creator might be in the way I die, in resignation not desperation.

Marriage

In this entry on page 2 of his journal, Ronald has been told about the diagnosis and realizes he must now tell Susie, his wife.

> Childhood sweethearts, we have been married for 40 years and are so close that it's sometimes hard to know where one of us ends and

the other begins. Yet neither of us is a passive personality, each has a full and separate life and each has several rooms in the head that the other has never entered or has visited only rarely. She still is full of surprises.

Today the closeness helps because, when I break the news, there's very little to be said. Each knows how the other feels. Each knows that self-pity is the greatest and deadliest of the luxuries. We keep ourselves well back from the precipice of uncontrolled emotion.

She expresses hope but agrees that the prospects are grim. Her face tells me she wishes I weren't driven to discuss the finalities so immediately, but she knows I must. So: Notes on funeral plans are in my pending file, honey, but they are only for guidance, subject to any change you want to make. So: I'm sure I want to be cremated. So: The insurance is okay but I'll get pension details. So: As usual, let's be open and get the word out right away to son John in Atlanta and daughter Susan in New Hampshire.

A few hugs, a few handclasps and the worst of the telling is over. I think of the country song about being married to the wrong woman and realize again how great it is to be married to the right one. Snarls, sneers and shouts; coldness, crying and crustiness; bullying, bravado and deceitful baloney. Check all of the above, for they have been a part of the marriage, and my mind cringes when I think of some of them. But those threads have failed to mar the huge glowing tapestry we have created over the years.

In the following entry, Ronald is lying in the hospital bed, unable to sleep, and decides to focus his mind on gratitude.

My mind speeds to our bedroom, sees her there under our blanket, brushes her hair, kisses her cheek, steps back—and remembers. That face has grown slack with mine, some of its lines created by me, but I can move it back in time, phase after phase like a film running backwards, into the preteen years when its color was rosy and its dimples winked with life. I know how it registers joy, anger, fear, and all the rest. I know the certain set look of determination, the lifted eyebrows of skepticism, the melting mien of warmth and trust.

In another entry, he talks about the voices he loves, including Susie's.

> I stop bellowing hymns in church sometimes and quietly listen to that voice beside me, remembering how we sang in a childhood octet together. I listen to her talk with someone else on the telephone, to her ways of expressing herself. . . . Too often I was more interested in what I was singing and saying.

Family

The family, somewhat scattered from New Hampshire to Iowa to Mississippi, rallied and began to call and visit, as you might imagine. This entry notes a quiet day with family.

> It has been a family day, Susie quietly addressing Christmas cards in the hospital room, John and Dee dropping by, Susan telephoning. What more could a man ask for than loving family and friends, a buddy, a good shower. . . . What indeed when he has been keeping notes by hand? "I'm dying to use a typewriter," I tell Susie and want to bite my tongue. "I'm dying . . ." is not the most diplomatic expression to use these days.

Ronald began to feel that the visits, the experiences with family, were offerings for him to treasure.

> Offerings. I've had them all day from others. Three grandgirls called from New Hampshire to sing their own version of Jingle Bells:
>
> "Jingle bells, jingle bells, jingle all the way,
> Why the heck is Grand Dad in the hospital today?
> Jingle bells, jingle bells, jingle all the way,
> We all love you Grand Dad and that's all we have to say."
>
> John brought a handmade gift from his daughter, Tricia, 3, a Santa Claus made at Sunday School, and a video tape of her throwing me a kiss . . . .
> Later we all go walking up the street and around the cul-de-sac, the two youngest children running and holding hands, the image of

happiness. Oh, it feels wonderful to walk outside again in the sunshine, stretching the muscles and working some of the stiffness from the hip joints.

Our first cousin, Douglas, who was like another brother to Ronald, squeezed in a quick visit from Mississippi.

And now Douglas is here to see me. He has driven 350 miles in the rain for a couple hours with me, and then he turns around and heads home again. We speak in shorthand, a few words that carry a lot of meaning and evoke a lot of laughs. An aura of woodsiness and family tradition and good humor surrounds him. It's as though he has brought part of my marrow for a visit.

Then this entry from day sixteen, New Year's Eve, 1981:

Paper hats and noisemakers . . . champagne and merrymakers . . . we have them all. Jimmy and Sally have brought them in and we're ready to move into that block of time known as 1982. We all meander through time as though heedless of Psalm 90, incorporated in Isaac Watts' great hymn:

"Time like an ever rolling stream
 Bears all its sons away,
They fly forgotten as a dream,
Dies at the opening day."

During the evening, Betty and Bubba Floyd, whom we have seen every New Year's Eve for many years, dropped by and had a little impromptu Stamps-Baxter shaped note gospel singing. Fun.

1982 is almost here. We put on party hats, open the champagne, and get ready. There's a sweetness, albeit bitter sweetness, to it all for me, the first time we have all spent New Year's Eve together, and doing so under adverse conditions brought on me, I want to be loudly cheerful but am too tired to be my typically exuberant self. Damn.

Yet, yet, when the moment of midnight comes, I am happy and joyous, and we all go into a songfest, led by John. . . . It's hard to express the pleasure I feel, sitting here singing with my family, from Susie on down to three-year-old Tricia. I see Jimmy and John sitting there, improvising jazz, and I know they will enjoy each other's company for years. I see the companionship that Ira and Susan feel with this, and it's pleasant to know that all of these people, so close to me, really like each other and feel comfortable with each other. I know they will be loving and supporting one another—John and Dee, Susan and Ira, Jimmy and Sally, and Susie—no matter what lies ahead. And I'm proud of all five grandchildren, scattered sleepily around the room, taking it all in.

Friends

This entry is from day two of the journal.

I lie awake in the pre-dawn darkness and think of family then switch to friends. Names and faces slide through my mind.

I could be apart from some of these characters for a thousand years and, seeing them again, would feel instant contact, a special spark, and would want to start talking immediately about a specific topic or recalling moments when, or spinning yarns.

With some I would want to discuss stubborn work problems we overcame together; with some, religion and church work; with some, fishing trips; with some, sailing trips; with some, how beautifully we sang when we stayed up drinking all night; with some, the splendor of the lies we told each other as we drove around in the pickup truck and drank beer, country music tumbling out the windows; with some, bird watching; and with others, people watching.

Some of the talk would be lofty; some if it petty and vicious. Honesty compels me to admit that I would enjoy both equally.

I lie here and wonder about any common thread in this collection of rare friends. There is none—good ole boys and feminists, political liberals and arch conservatives, preachers and atheists, teetotalers and drinkers are all in the mix. And I wouldn't rank the joys of beery pickup truck riding any higher or lower than the quiet theology talks; the times at symphonic concerts against friends joining me in singing shaped note gospel music; sun-kissed cruises against a catchless trout fishing trip in a chilly mountain wilderness; a trip to England against a visit in the neighborhood.

Out of many friends, these are special, even though I see some of them rarely. I ought to go out of my way to say goodbye to them in a letter they will receive after I depart. I need to unpack before I go, and that letter will let me unload a lot of thanks.

Work

Ronald was a newspaperman and proud of it. He spent his career with the Associated Press, and at his "retirement," he was bureau chief in Atlanta and was the senior AP bureau chief in the world. He had started at the bottom and worked his way almost to the top. It is no surprise, then, that his journal would include reflections on his work.

It's funny that as a green rookie you start with an organization and you scramble to get a footing and, after a while, you aren't so green anymore. You're a statehouse reporter and you wonder if you could run a small office. And you do and you wonder if you could make it as a newsman in New York. And you do and they offer you a state news operation to run in an area of fierce competition. And you do okay in New Jersey so they offer you Connecticut as the guy in charge.

All along, there are all those "what if's"—what if this kind of story or staff situation develops, what if, what if? All of the what ifs develop and so do you, in Connecticut, and when they send you to Atlanta in 1963 at the height of civil rights changes, the same things happen. All of the what ifs. Somehow you make it through, sometimes blunderingly. At times the work impinges too heavily on personal life and affects the family but you blunder through. Suddenly you realize you no longer are a rookie—you are a damned old bull moose, afraid of nothing professionally.

Two questions have never haunted me: Do I like my job? Do I consider it important to society?

I can't remember a day when I dreaded going to work, whether it was a routine news day or a day of immense pressure writing a story of intense worldwide interest.

Then, commenting further on his work, he expresses what I consider gratitude for his passion in life.

I can cope with diminished physical passion, this person who spent a lifetime of macho-ism before seeing its ridiculous aspects, far better than I could with the loss of a passionate heart and mind. . . .

Give me passionate reporters, passionate doctors, passionate preachers, passionate politicians—people who really *care* about things. They're the ones who have helped civilization creep upward.

At one point I told Ronald that all the messages he was receiving seemed like farewell messages, creating an aura of impending death.

Referring to me, he wrote, "He cited a telegram I received this morning informing me that the AP Board of Directors had passed a resolution commending my work over the years, a commendation that I treasure highly. I told him I understood his point but that I wouldn't have turned aside a single letter or gesture. It wasn't that people were giving up on me so much as they wanted to make sure that I knew they cared for me."

Observations and Reflections on His Illness

This was an early entry from the hospital, soon after the diagnosis.

> . . . As I shuffle from the bathroom pushing my IV stick, suddenly there's beautiful music floating through the corridors of this cancer ward, Christmas carols. It's coming closer. Several hospital employees, wearing their work clothes, have changed roles and become professional-sounding singers. . . . The healers of wounded bodies now are singing to the wounded spirits and doing so on their lunch hour.

Among Ronald's serious observations, he inserted humorous asides throughout the journal, another sign of his spirit.

> Christmas Day. When one has a—nope. I'm not going to say it. I have spent an entire career avoiding "one" sentences. One what— horse, turkey, human being, poltergeist? Restart.
>
> When you have a life-threatening illness, the days no longer pass like dry leaves in a gale, uncounted and unheeded. Instead they are individual glasses of rare wines, to be sipped and savored.

Doubly so, then, is Christmas in this context. I savor this rare wine as though it may not be tasted again but with pleasure and exhilaration as befits a wine of quality.

Then, on the day after Christmas, more humor:

I've had this tickling in my throat and a cough since the day I entered the hospital, the result of too much dry air there. It's merely a nuisance and nobody seems to be able to solve it. Today *I* make the diagnosis: kennel cough, the ailment that our dog gets when she spends time in a kennel and barks too much. I decided I may go to the vet for treatment if I don't get it cleared up. Sure would make for an interesting health insurance claim. Are you listening, Prudential?

In Conclusion

I confess, dear readers that, even after thirty years, this has been a difficult essay to write. I close with three more entries, the first of which came after Ronald and Susie spent a while looking at a collection of photographs.

I wanted to break into a dance of joy. What a wonderful life it has been, what good fortune has touched me and my family at almost every turn—and it's not over yet. Even now I keep receiving letters telling me what a splendid fellow I am. If they keep coming I soon will be forced to conclude one of two things—either they are telling the truth or they are convinced I'm a goner. Meantime, I'm assuming nothing—and appreciating the hell out of all those golden, gorgeous words . . . .

Throughout this journey, I have felt a certain buoyancy as if I were a sort of airfoil being continuously lifted by the warm air of prayers, good wishes, and friendship. That ain't bull, Pardner. I actually felt it.

Then, finally, there is this entry toward the end of the journal:

Snow covered everything today, and we had a spectacular display of cardinals, goldfinches, towhees, and other songbirds. It all served as a metaphor—a temporarily bleak outlook but one with many birds of hope.

Gratitude indeed.

Living with Regret

When I first heard the Buddhist saying that regret is the most wasted emotion, I thought, "That's right. Don't look back at what you did wrong or failed to do; look ahead at what to do now."

While that's good advice, I now think it goes only so far. I'm now not so sure that regret is a wasted emotion. Like it or not, regret happens, and we shouldn't view it so negatively. We've often been taught that regret, like grief, is something to put behind us, to get past, to treat as if it's an enemy of our well-being.

But it's not so easy to let go of or get rid of regret. In fact, regret may be one of the most difficult feelings to put behind us. Let me venture an opinion that you, right now, can remember and still regret something from many years ago, perhaps even from childhood. If so, you have plenty of company, including me.

> *The best way to show my gratitude to God is to accept everything, even my problems, with joy.*
>
> —MOTHER TERESA
> (1910–1997)

It is rare when a person does not, at some time or another, feel regret. It seems to me there are three attitudes we can have about regret: we can treat it like a character flaw and try to overcome it; we can become so preoccupied with it that we begin to wallow in it; or we can face it, examine it, and learn from it. Obviously we should develop the third attitude.

It begins with redefining regret from a negative feeling to a source of positive understanding and action. Approached with that attitude, regret demonstrates that you are a good enough person to acknowledge, at least to yourself, whatever you regret. In many cases, it demonstrates that you have a conscience.

Next comes being grateful that we always have another chance and that we don't have to be stuck in our regret. The objective is to be able to live *with* regret without living *in* regret.

In the past several years, I have conducted workshops on leadership with various kinds of organizations: business, education, nonprofit, political. In trying to emphasize self-awareness as a characteristic of leadership, I've had participants address directly the regret in their lives.

I suggest to them, as I do now to you, that the kinds of regret boil down to this: regret for what I did that I ought not to have done, and regret for what I did not do that I ought to have done.

Most of the time this means what I said or didn't say; what I did or didn't do; or the manner in which I said or didn't say, or did or didn't do whatever it was—in other words, the what and the how of my behavior.

I begin by asking them to write a yes or no answer to these questions:

Could I have been a better . . .

Father or mother?

Husband or wife?

Friend?

Boss?

Employee?

Citizen?

Then I ask them to ponder those questions, asking themselves, "How?" I let them do this privately without sharing the answers with the group. I am trying stimulate introspection.

The next exercise is to ask the participants to list the things they regret doing, actually writing out, "I regret saying_____" or "I regret doing_____." Then I ask them to write what they feel when thinking about what they said or did. Embarrassment? Anger at themselves?

Then I ask them to write down the consequences or perceived consequences of their words or actions. They follow that by writing what they should have done instead (perhaps nothing) or what they should have said (perhaps nothing.)

Next to last, I ask them to write the lessons they learned, including what they will do or not do if there's a next time.

And finally the last big question: "Is there something I should do now to change or mitigate those consequences?" In Alcoholics Anonymous and other twelve-step programs, they call this "making amends." In church, we call it "asking forgiveness."

If you'll try these exercises, you'll find that the process is a gift to yourself. Making amends is a gift to yourself. Asking forgiveness is a gift to yourself.

That gift is the peace of mind as well as the knowledge that, if the same situation arises again, you will do or say things differently. Accept that gift with gratitude and move on.

Moment of Gratitude

Last Breath

Several years ago, I was making my annual strategic planning presentation to the president and CEO of the corporation that employed me. It was an important meeting and, as you might imagine, somewhat formal.

My secretary entered the room quietly and handed me a note: "Red is fading fast."

It meant that my colleague and dear friend, Red Seney, was dying at the hospital where he'd been hanging on in his final struggle with bone marrow cancer.

The timing was not good. I felt enormous pressure to continue the meeting, but I said, "Please excuse me. Red Seney's dying now and I need to go to the hospital," then I asked one of my senior associates to continue the presentation on my behalf.

When I arrived at the hospital room, Red's eyes widened in recognition, and then within a few minutes he took his last breath.

I was so grateful for that final look of recognition from Red and the knowledge that we'd connected one last time.

Poems

Disconnected
(Ten years after the death of my brother)
How could I have explained
to the woman who answered
that I dialed not to reach her
but just to dial
that very number
as I have so many times before
to hear it ring once again
and remember for a moment
a voice I'll never hear again?

Ronald's Dance
Only he and I know that he is Gene Nelson
in *Oklahoma*; to everyone else
he is the strange kid dancing,
wild jerky arms swinging
spinning stomping jumping and twirling,
while the other dancers clap and laugh,
some with him some at him,
and I am seized by that terrible sense
of discovery and loss that accompanies
every new thing I see Ronald do.
Even now while in his mind everyone is celebrating
the exuberance and abandon of Gene Nelson
dancing on top of the railroad cars
I can't forget
that the train is pulling out of the station.

Section Seven
The Gratitude Inventory

My Gratitude Inventory

Part of loving the life we have means living in the present and loving the life we have *now*, not the life we used to have or the life we're going to have. So I suggest that you and I take an inventory of the things for which we're grateful. I've arbitrarily created some categories. You can use mine or create your own.

I'll go first.

Family and Friends
• My wife, Sally, with whom I have recently celebrated our thirtieth wedding anniversary and have an utterly committed and loving relationship.
• Our son with autism, Ronald, who is doing so well, has a job, lives on his own, drives a car, is a member of the church, and is a very upbeat and likeable person.
• My son Rick, who has been so successful working as an attorney for the rights of others, has become an author, and makes time to have lunch with me almost every week. He also has given me two fine grandsons, both of whom are doing schoolwork of a complexity that makes me happy I'm not still in school.
• My son Jim Jr., who, after many difficult years, has overcome his addictions, has a good job, is making music again, has lunch with me regularly, and participates with the family in ways he's not done in years.
• My in-laws, who are among my life's great blessings. I didn't know that any family could be so loving toward one another.

• Loving friendships that grow richer by the years, that are nurtured by common experiences of celebration as well as mourning, of joy as well as sadness. Friends have taught me and continue to teach me so much.

Community

• Plymouth Congregational United Church of Christ in Des Moines, Iowa. I love this community of faith, and nothing describes it better than the church motto: "We agree to differ; we resolve to love; we unite to serve."

• Ministers, not specifically of any denomination, who work hard every day at leading their congregations.

• Theologians and others who devote themselves to biblical scholarship.

• All the caregivers and friends who've helped Ronald over the years.

• The friendly and helpful drivers of the Des Moines metro buses who I know keep an eye on Ronald.

• Schoolteachers, particularly special education teachers. It seems everyone has ideas about how teachers should do their jobs, but few critics offer to change places with them.

> *As we express our gratitude, we must never forget that the highest appreciation is not to utter words, but to live by them.*
>
> —JOHN F. KENNEDY
> (1917–1963)

• The law enforcement, firefighters, and other "first responders."

• The military people who get a lot of criticism but who work hard to accomplish the missions they are assigned.

• Government workers who, despite being almost constantly maligned, are in my experience dedicated and hard working, and whose efforts lubricate the sometimes creaky wheels of our public institutions.

• Our elected officials. Yes, believe it or not, I'm grateful for all of them, of whatever party, because theirs is a demanding and often thankless job.

• Our country. Who doesn't have criticisms? But I am grateful that I was born into and live in this country despite all its struggles.

Work

• Two successful careers, one before I retired and another after I retired. I'm grateful for all the opportunities I've had as an author and speaker to travel in this country and others, to meet many interesting and wonderful people who are, in their own way, trying to make a difference.

• Opportunities to use my skills volunteering for disability rights groups, educational institutions, and the arts, where I've learned as much as I did in my career.

Play

• The Internet, believe it or not, that provides the means for staying in touch with widely scattered friends and loved ones, for exchanging jokes and music and photos.

• Many hours of sheer pleasure jamming with my friends in a musical group we call—because all of us are long of tooth—the Over the Hill Jazz Band.

• Fishing excursions on the Mississippi River south of Memphis with my friend Sam Gore in his boat, *The Death Wish II*.

• Poetry and all forms of literature. Music and art.

Obviously, this is an incomplete list, and if I gave it more thought, I could fill another page. But those would just be expansions or slightly different versions of what I've already covered.

Next, I invite you to make your own inventory.

Your Gratitude Inventory

Now it's your turn.

I've left the next pages blank so you can contribute to this book by listing why you're grateful. Create your own categories or use the ones I named on the previous pages: Family, Friends, Community, Work, Play.

Add your own categories. For instance, instead of making church and faith part of "community," as I did, you might want those to be a separate category.

Or, if you participate in the arts, you might want that to be a separate category aside from "play."

The point in making this list is not simply to make a list but to take time to reflect on gratitude. As the old Sunday school song said, "Count your blessings, name them one by one . . . ."

Then I suggest you share this list with family and loved ones and invite them to make a similar list. This may even start a movement of people taking time to be grateful and counting their blessings.

One Final Question

As you begin your own gratitude list, ponder this question: If you had but one day to live, to whom would you express gratitude—and why aren't you doing it today?

Why I Am Grateful

Why I Am Grateful

Why I Am Grateful

Other available titles from SMYTH & HELWYS®

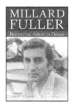

Beyond the American Dream
Millard Fuller

In 1968, Millard finished the story of his journey from pauper to millionaire to home builder. His wife, Linda, occasionally would ask him about getting it published, but Millard would reply, "Not now. I'm too busy." This is that story. *978-1-57312-563-5 272 pages/pb* **$20.00**

The Black Church
Relevant or Irrelevant in the 21st Century?
Reginald F. Davis

The Black Church contends that a relevant church struggles to correct oppression, not maintain it. How can the black church focus on the liberation of the black community, thereby reclaiming the loyalty and respect of the black community? *978-1-57312-557-4 144 pages/pb* **$15.00**

Blissful Affliction
The Ministry and Misery of Writing
Judson Edwards

Edwards draws from more than forty years of writing experience to explore why we use the written word to change lives and how to improve the writing craft. *978-1-57312-594-9 144 pages/pb* **$15.00**

Bottom Line Beliefs
Twelve Doctrines All Christians Hold in Common (Sort of)
Michael B. Brown

Despite our differences, there are principles that are bedrock to the Christian faith. These are the subject of Michael Brown's *Bottom Line Beliefs*. *978-1-57312-520-8 112 pages/pb* **$15.00**

Christian Civility in an Uncivil World
Mitch Carnell, ed.

When we encounter a Christian who thinks and believes differently, we often experience that difference as an attack on the principles upon which we have built our lives and as a betrayal to the faith. However, it is possible for Christians to retain their differences and yet unite in respect for each other. It is possible to love one another and at the same time retain our individual beliefs. *978-1-57312-537-6 160 pages/pb* **$17.00**

To order call **1-800-747-3016** or visit **www.helwys.com**

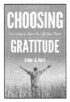

Choosing Gratitude
Learning to Love the Life You Have

James A. Autry

Autry reminds us that gratitude is a choice, a spiritual—not social—process. He suggests that if we cultivate gratitude as a way of being, we may not change the world and its ills, but we can change our response to the world. If we fill our lives with moments of gratitude, we will indeed love the life we have.   *978-1-57312-614-4 144 pages/pb* **$15.00**

Contextualizing the Gospel
A Homiletic Commentary on 1 Corinthians

Brian L. Harbour

Harbour examines every part of Paul's letter, providing a rich resource for those who want to struggle with the difficult texts as well as the simple texts, who want to know how God's word—all of it—intersects with their lives today.   *978-1-57312-589-5 240 pages/pb* **$19.00**

Dance Lessons
Moving to the Beat of God's Heart

Jeanie Miley

Miley shares her joys and struggles a she learns to "dance" with the Spirit of the Living God.   *978-1-57312-622-9 240 pages/pb* **$19.00**

The Disturbing Galilean
Essays About Jesus

Malcolm Tolbert

In this captivating collection of essays, Dr. Malcolm Tolbert reflects on nearly two dozen stories taken largely from the Synoptic Gospels. Those stories range from Jesus' birth, temptation, teaching, anguish at Gethsemane, and crucifixion.   *978-1-57312-530-7 140 pages/pb* **$15.00**

Divorce Ministry
A Guidebook

Charles Qualls

This book shares with the reader the value of establishing a divorce recovery ministry while also offering practical insights on establishing your own unique church-affiliated program. Whether you are working individually with one divorced person or leading a large group, *Divorce Ministry: A Guidebook* provides helpful resources to guide you through the emotional and relational issues divorced people often encounter.

978-1-57312-588-8 156 pages/pb **$16.00**

The Enoch Factor
The Sacred Art of Knowing God

Stephen McSwain

The Enoch Factor is a persuasive argument for a more enlightened religious dialogue in America, one that affirms the goals of all religions—guiding followers in self-awareness, finding serenity and happiness, and discovering what the author describes as "the sacred art of knowing God." 978-1-57312-556-7 256 pages/pb **$21.00**

Faith Postures
Cultivating Christian Mindfulness

Holly Sprink

Sprink guides readers through her own growing awareness of God's desire for relationship and of developing the emotional, physical, spiritual postures that enable us to learn to be still, to listen, to be mindful of the One outside ourselves. 1-978-57312-547-5 160 pages/pb **$16.00**

The Good News According to Jesus
A New Kind of Christianity for a New Kind of Christian

Chuck Queen

In The Good News According to Jesus, Chuck Queen contends that when we broaden our study of Jesus, the result is a richer, deeper, healthier, more relevant and holistic gospel, a Christianity that can transform this world into God's new world.
978-1-57312-528-4 216 pages/pb **$18.00**

Healing Our Hurts
Coping with Difficult Emotions

Daniel Bagby

In Healing Our Hurts, Daniel Bagby identifies and explains all the dynamics at play in these complex emotions. Offering practical biblical insights to these feelings, he interprets faith-based responses to separate overly religious piety from true, natural human emotion. This book helps us learn how to deal with life's difficult emotions in a redemptive and responsible way. 978-1-57312-613-7 144 pages/pb **$15.00**

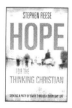

Hope for the Thinking Christian
Seeking a Path of Faith through Everyday Life

Stephen Reese

Readers who want to confront their faith more directly, to think it through and be open to God in an individual, authentic, spiritual encounter will find a resonant voice in Stephen Reese.
978-1-57312-553-6 160 pages/pb **$16.00**

Hoping Liberia
Stories of Civil War from Africa's First Republic
John Michael Helms

Through historical narrative, theological ponderings, personal confession, and thoughtful questions, Helms immerses readers into a period of political turmoil and violence, a devastating civil war, and the immeasurable suffering experienced by the Liberian people.

978-1-57312-544-4 208 pages/pb **$18.00**

James (Smyth & Helwys Annual Bible Study series)
Being Right in a Wrong World
Michael D. McCullar

Unlike Paul, who wrote primarily to congregations defined by Gentile believers, James wrote to a dispersed and persecuted fellowship of Hebrew Christians who would soon endure even more difficulty in the coming years.

Teaching Guide 1-57312-604-5 160 pages/ pb **$14.00**
Study Guide 1-57312-605-2 96 pages/pb **$6.00**

James M. Dunn and Soul Freedom
Aaron Douglas Weaver

James Milton Dunn, over the last fifty years, has been the most aggressive Baptist proponent for religious liberty in the United States. Soul freedom—voluntary uncoerced faith and an unfettered individual conscience before God—is the basis of his understanding of church-state separation and the historic Baptist basis of religious liberty.

978-1-57312-590-1 224 pages/pb **$18.00**

The Jesus Tribe
Following Christ in the Land of the Empire
Ronnie McBrayer

The Jesus Tribe fleshes out the implications, possibilities, contradictions, and complexities of what it means to live within the Jesus Tribe and in the shadow of the American Empire.

978-1-57312-592-5 208 pages/pb **$17.00**

Joint Venture
Jeanie Miley

Joint Venture is a memoir of the author's journey to find and express her inner, authentic self, not as an egotistical venture, but as a sacred responsibility and partnership with God. Miley's quest for Christian wholeness is a rich resource for other seekers.

978-1-57312-581-9 224 pages/pb **$17.00**

Let Me More of Their Beauty See

Reading Familiar Verses in Context

Diane G. Chen

Let Me More of Their Beauty See offers eight examples of how attention to the historical and literary settings can safeguard against taking a text out of context, bring out its transforming power in greater dimension, and help us apply Scripture appropriately in our daily lives.

978-1-57312-564-2 160 pages/pb **$17.00**

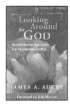

Looking Around for God

The Strangely Reverent Observations of an Unconventional Christian

James A. Autry

Looking Around for God, Autry's tenth book, is in many ways his most personal. In it he considers his unique life of faith and belief in God. Autry is a former Fortune 500 executive, author, poet, and consultant whose work has had a significant influence on leadership thinking.

978-157312-484-3 144 pages/pb **$16.00**

Maggie Lee for Good

Jinny and John Hinson

Maggie Lee for Good captures the essence of a young girl's boundless faith and spirit. Her parents' moving story of the accident that took her life will inspire readers who are facing loss, looking for evidence of God's sustaining grace, or searching for ways to make a meaningful difference in the lives of others.
978-1-57312-630-4 144 pages/pb **$15.00**

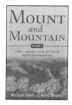

Mount and Mountain

Vol. 1: A Reverend and a Rabbi Talk About the Ten Commandments

Rami Shapiro and Michael Smith

Mount and Mountain represents the first half of an interfaith dialogue—a dialogue that neither preaches nor placates but challenges its participants to work both singly and together in the task of reinterpreting sacred texts. Mike and Rami discuss the nature of divinity, the power of faith, the beauty of myth and story, the necessity of doubt, the achievements, failings, and future of religion, and, above all, the struggle to live ethically and in harmony with the way of God.
978-1-57312-612-0 144 pages/pb **$15.00**

Overcoming Adolescence
Growing Beyond Childhood into Maturity
Marion D. Aldridge

In *Overcoming Adolescence*, Marion Aldridge poses questions for adults of all ages to consider. His challenge to readers is one he has personally worked to confront: to grow up *all the way*—mentally, physically, academically, socially, emotionally, and spiritually. The key not only involves knowing how to work through the process, but how to recognize what may be contributing to our perpetual adolescence.

978-1-57312-577-2 156 pages/pb **$17.00**

Psychic Pancakes & Communion Pizza
More Musings and Mutterings of a Church Misfit
Bert Montgomery

Psychic Pancakes & Communion Pizza is Bert Montgomery's highly anticipated follow-up to *Elvis, Willie, Jesus & Me* and contains further reflections on music, film, culture, life, and finding Jesus in the midst of it all. *978-1-57312-576-9 160 pages/pb* **$16.00**

Reading Job (Reading the Old Testament series)
A Literary and Theological Commentary
James L. Crenshaw

At issue in the Book of Job is a question with which most all of us struggle at some point in life, "Why do bad things happen to good people?" James Crenshaw has devoted his life to studying the disturbing matter of theodicy—divine justice—that troubles many people of faith.

978-1-57312-574-1 192 pages/pb **$22.00**

Reading Samuel (Reading the Old Testament series)
A Literary and Theological Commentary
Johanna W. H. van Wijk-Bos

Interpreted masterfully by preeminent Old Testament scholar Johanna W. H. van Wijk-Bos, the story of Samuel touches on a vast array of subjects that make up the rich fabric of human life. The reader gains an inside look at leadership, royal intrigue, military campaigns, occult practices, and the significance of religious objects of veneration.

978-1-57312-607-6 272 pages/pb **$22.00**

The Role of the Minister in a Dying Congregation
Lynwood B. Jenkins

In *The Role of the Minister in a Dying Congregation* Jenkins provides a courageous and responsible resource on one of the most critical issues in congregational life: how to help a congregation conclude its ministry life cycle with dignity and meaning.

978-1-57312-571-0 96 pages/pb **$14.00**

Sessions with Philippians (Session Bible Studies series)
Finding Joy in Community

Bo Prosser

In this brief letter to the Philippians, Paul makes clear the centrality of his faith in Jesus Christ, his love for the Philippian church, and his joy in serving both Christ and their church.

978-1-57312-579-6 112 pages/pb **$13.00**

Sessions with Samuel (Session Bible Studies series)
Stories from the Edge

Tony W. Cartledge

In these stories, Israel faces one crisis after another, a people constantly on the edge. Individuals like Saul and David find themselves on the edge as well, facing troubles of leadership and personal struggle. Yet, each crisis becomes a gateway for learning that God is always present, that hope remains.

978-1-57312-555-0 112 pages/pb **$13.00**

Silver Linings
My Life Before and After Challenger 7

June Scobee Rodgers

We know the public story of *Challenger 7*'s tragic destruction. That day, June's life took a new direction that ultimately led to the creation of the Challenger Center and to new life and new love. Her story of Christian faith and triumph over adversity will inspire readers of every age.

978-1-57312-570-3 352 pages/hc **$28.00**

Telling the Story
The Gospel in a Technological Age

J. Stanley Hargraves

From the advent of the printing press to modern church buildings with LCD projectors and computers, the church has adapted the means of communicating the gospel. Adapting that message to the available technology helps the church reach out in meaningful ways to people around the world.

978-1-57312-550-5 112 pages/pb **$14.00**

This is What a Preacher Looks Like
Sermons by Baptist Women in Ministry

Pamela Durso, ed.

A collection of sermons by thirty-six Baptist women, their voices are soft and loud, prophetic and pastoral, humorous and sincere. They are African American, Asian, Latina, and Caucasian. They are sisters, wives, mothers, grandmothers, aunts, and friends.

978-1-57312-554-3 144 pages/pb **$18.00**

To Be a Good and Faithful Servant
The Life and Work of a Minister

Cecil Sherman

This book offers a window into how one pastor navigated the many daily challenges and opportunities of ministerial life and shares that wisdom with church leaders wherever they are in life—whether serving as lay leaders or as ministers just out of seminary, midway through a career, or seeking renewal after many years of service.　978-1-57312-559-8 208 pages/pb **$20.00**

Transformational Leadership
Leading with Integrity

Charles B. Bugg

"Transformational" leadership involves understanding and growing so that we can help create positive change in the world. This book encourages leaders to be willing to change if *they* want to help transform the world. They are honest about their personal strengths and weaknesses, and are not afraid of doing a fearless moral inventory of themselves.

978-1-57312-558-1 112 pages/pb **$14.00**

Written on My Heart
Daily Devotions for Your Journey through the Bible

Ann H. Smith

Smith takes readers on a fresh and exciting journey of daily readings of the Bible that will change, surprise, and renew you.

978-1-57312-549-9 288 pages/pb **$18.00**

When Crisis Comes Home
Revised and Expanded

John Lepper

The Bible is full of examples of how God's people, with homes grounded in the faith, faced crisis after crisis. These biblical personalities and families were not hopeless in the face of catastrophe—instead, their faith in God buoyed them, giving them hope for the future and strength to cope in the present. John Lepper will help you and your family prepare for, deal with, and learn from crises in your home. *978-1-57312-539-0 152 pages/pb* **$17.00**

Cecil Sherman Formations Commentary

Add the wit and wisdom of Cecil Sherman to your library. After 15 years of writing the Smyth & Helwys Formations Commentary, you can now purchase the 5-volume compilation covering the best of Cecil Sherman from Genesis to Revelation.

Vol. 1: Genesis–Job   *1-57312-476-1 208 pages/pb* **$17.00**
Vol. 2: Psalms–Malachi   *1-57312-477-X 208 pages/pb* **$17.00**
Vol. 3: Matthew–Mark   *1-57312-478-8 208 pages/pb* **$17.00**
Vol. 4: Luke–Acts   *1-57312-479-6 208 pages/pb* **$17.00**
Vol. 5: Romans–Revelation   *1-57312-480-X 208 pages/pb* **$17.00**

Also from James Autry

The Spirit of Retirement
Creating a Life of Meaning and Personal Growth

Poet, author, and Fortune 500 executive, Autry challenges readers to take advantage of the many opportunities that come with retirement. Addressing issues such as transition, direction, developing relationships and yourself, Autry makes it clear that retirement can be a unique and special time.

Retail Price $19.99 • **Your Price $15.99**

Looking Around for God
The Oddly Reverent Observations of an Unconventional Christian

I loved this book! Sweeping aside conventional pieties, Jim Autry's clear insights, told with wit and poetry, show how we may see traces of the divine shining through our everyday world.

— Elaine Pagels
Harrington Professor of Religion
Princeton University

Retail Price $16.00 • **Your Price $12.80**

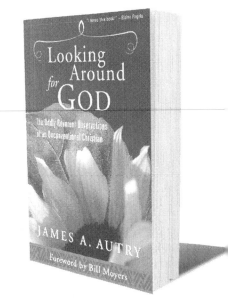

Call 1.800.747.3016 to order • For more information, visit www.helwys.com